THE DOITGIRL DIARIES.

Vol. 1

by Sarah Durham Wilson

2011- 2014

I stand

At the threshold.

And this is where I release

All that is old

And that is how

one becomes bold

And enters the new story

That is longing

to be told.

**

Below, a collection of my thoughts and experiences in four years as a student of the earth, because everyone's story deserves to be told, and no one can tell anyone

they sing their own song wrong.

**

Late Summer 2011, Kripalu, The Berkshires.

Thanks for the Rain.

Sometimes I still think I'm a Wendy.

Wendy was me, and so many wonderful women I have known who wait behind the glass of life. I can still be a Wendy.

Wendy is a wait-er and not a live-er.

Wendy was me in my relationship with my ex. Wendy waits by the fire, on the couch for Peter Pan to fly home and tell her all about her adventures. Wendy sits by the window and waits for him to tell her about life, looking out, growing a bit resentful, growing a bit bitter, growing ever more brittle, waiting. Waiting makes us bitter. Waiting makes us brittle. And when we are bitter and brittle, we break. She waits for

Peter to have his adventures and triumphs, waits for Peter to tell her about living. Eventually Wendy gets old and dies by the fire, waiting for Peter, and Peter in turn, forgets about her. He's too busy living to remember.

When I talked to my ex last night, he was packing for tour. He was always leaving for tour, and I never got to the point where I couldn't take it personally. The bed always felt as wide and empty as the Sahara. So did my days. Hence all that wine I drowned in to quench my undying thirst, for him, for my own adventures, for my true purpose.

But maybe this Wendy finally got free.

Break the Glass, the wall between you and life, the window of pain and fear and self-doubt that stands between you and your life and dreams. You have to act, to free Wendy, to punch through the fantasy and touch the reality. Reach down and grab her from the floor and take her through the window with you. You have to punch through the wall of fantasy to touch the heart of life and let your heart be touched by life. To Free Wendy. Have your own stories, scars, failures, triumphs, successes. As Rumi says, "unfold your own myth." Don't leave it up to others to live for you, to choose for you, to tell you about life. Stop just dreaming, and act out your dreams.

I woke up with the tears, but I woke up in my own safe bed in my own chosen town on my own adventure.

The last time I cried this hard about him, I woke up on the other coast, with a horrible hangover, with my wedding dress boxed up to be sent back, next to a small trashcan he had stuffed with the wedding invitations.

What you have survived really has made you stronger. Don't forget what your soul and spirit have overcome. Don't forget what you've faced, how you've grown, what you've learned, who you are, and what you are capable of. Your strength, your survival, your endless warrior spirit should make you fearless. Nothing has stopped you yet.

Phoenixes rise from the fire, burned down to the eternal core of who they truly are.

Oh, and heroes, they leave the house.

[SHE'S GOT THAT WHOLE

EARTH GODDESS WARRIOR PRIESTESS

GONNA SAVE THE WORLD VIBE.]

Fall, 2011. The Berkshires.

Grace in Omaha, Nebraska.

When I moved to Omaha in my mid-twenties, I moved with blind love for a man I had met late one night in the East Village. I had abandoned my journalism career in New York which no longer lit my fire, and for a brief, brilliantly new moment, I had a whole new life to fill in, a blank slate before all my old problems and fears map-quested and set out for me, like a dark bandwagon on my heels. Back then, I actually thought you could escape yourself.

A week or two into my move, my boyfriend was practicing with his band, and I was sitting alone in my new house blocks from Omaha's downtown, "Today, I'll get a dog,"

I said. I had always thought, if I was going to abandon New York for a quieter life, I would finally get a dog. I wanted a Subaru, and a dog. Then, I thought, everything would fall into place. How simple.

So I found my dog, which is a story in its own, for at the shelter they deemed her "unadoptable." She was emaciated, abused, with a bb bullet in her ear, and a snarl for every unfamiliar man. And I named her "Grace," without a hint of what that was. It was so difficult at first, this dog and her needs in my life. I was a party girl from NYC, with no routine or structure of my own, who had lived on expense accounts and interviewed rock stars and movie stars for a living, and now I was in the plains of Nebraska with this living, messy, needy being with as much baggage as me. I had never taken care of myself, let alone something outside of me. Her need mirrored my own. Vast, empty, unrelenting. I couldn't bare to look at it. I resented her need as much as my own. We were a mess. To think of this now makes me gasp, but for days after I adopted her I wanted to take her back. She was too real. "Who was I to care for another life," I thought, when I could barely care for my own?

And one day, less than a week later, she had had enough. And I will never forget the terror of that morning. She slipped out the front screen door and ran away, shooting across the streets of my new neighborhood, and she vanished. For twenty minutes or so I ran around like a crazy person, calling and screaming for her, and then I stopped and my crying stopped. "Gracie," I croaked her name, hunched over, winded on the sidewalk. As it was increasingly my nature, I gave up. Maybe this was supposed to happen. Maybe she was right to run away from me. Maybe, it was possible, she was doing us both a favor. Maybe the streets she knew so well were safer than my care.

I called out one last "Grace?"

Because she is built like a baby wolf, I saw only the fluff of her tail first, and then, like an old western movie show down, she appeared halfway down the sidewalk, her thick black toe nails clicking carefully on the cement. She came a bit closer to me, to really get a look at me, and then she stopped, a block away, and it was a stand off. I held my breath. She was sizing me up. Just two strays, sizing each other up.

People were watching this girl and her dog on that fall day as the leaves skittered across the streets. She was taking her time deciding, weighing her options. At least someone was breathing and taking a moment.

And it was an endless frozen moment, in which she could dart away forever at any second. Any sudden move of mine could send her running again. And if I had been her, I might have. But finally, in an act of Grace, she moved toward me, one spindly leg pushing forward after another. And then she trotted, carefully, back toward the house, past me, very dignified. She just walked into the house and I followed. And things were different then, because she had chosen me.

I was so used to being abandoned, left behind, and so was she. So as soon as things seemed unsafe, she ran before it could happen again. And I understood that. I was sure I knew how that morning would turn out: catastrophic. But she came back to me anyway, and there has never been doubt for either one of us ever again that we belong to each other and are in this together. That act of faith has made all the difference. Someone once told me that if you tell someone "I trust you," they won't lie to you. But that they need to feel trusted to be trustworthy. Gracie showed me she trusted me, and so I trusted myself to care for her.

RESCUES. Sometimes she still flinches/ when you reach out to touch her. /Sometimes she still barks when you're only trying to help/ Sometimes she'll even bare her teeth if you get too close to her wound. /It's true, My rescue and I are not that different. /No she's a mirror of a feral creature/ still learning what love is. /We've both been saved/ we've both been found/ we got our second chances. But somedays, some nights, it's a little too easy- no matter how hard life tries to remind us- to forget. And then we remember/ which always comes on the heels of the forgetting / like day always following night found, following lost- and we look around in wonder / that we no longer have to wander/ that we are home/in a home and we are safe and - most astonishing of all- loved.

Late Fall, 2011. Kripalu, The Berkshires.

Tell Yourself You're Beautiful.

In a Reiki course I took, we were talking about how our bodies and souls hold on to old loves, long after we feel we're supposed to be "over it." One fiery, compassionate, curious woman in my course, we'll call her Sheila, was newly liberated from her chains to an old ex. Do you ever feel you're walking around shackled by chains of your past? This unshackling process, despite her being happily married to someone else, had taken years, decades even.

He had been one of those breathless loves whom she found herself standing on the brink of her whole life for, conceding all she'd built and knew she was for him. But it was just that sort of love. A Learning Love. Because then, as it goes, bam- he was gone, and what we are left with are the lessons. They all end, all these love stories, until the one that doesn't.

Decades later, Shelia confronted him on the phone, and finally released him for good. After telling us the story, she chirped, "I feel great now!"

"But you know what makes me the angriest and saddest, is that when I got up the courage to look at old photos of us—in which I used to only notice him, like the sun, you couldn't look away. Anyway this time, when I was over him, I saw how BEAUTIFUL I was. I was always so worried I wasn't pretty enough for him, but I was more than pretty enough, I was beautiful! "

"Now looking back, I see the truth: I WAS SO BEAUTIFUL. Just as beautiful as him, he just had way more confidence than I did. He knew he was, and acted like, a total catch. Like life for him was full of infinite possibility. And that was the only difference between us, he believed it about himself, he knew this about himself, but I did not. This makes me so sad," she said. "I wish I had told myself everyday. Every day."

She reminded us to See yourself through the eyes of God, the eyes of Love. Divinely Perfect. I too look back at all the pictures of myself I hated at the time, now I see, I was young. I was beautiful. I was perfect. I wish I had known then, what I know now. So know it now. You were beautiful then and you are beautiful now.

[SHE SAID. She said, I want a gentleman. That's right a gentle, man. And she decided she no longer had time/ For those who didn't have time for her/ And that was it/ And that was that/ And that was all.]

Winter, 2011.

Free Union, Virginia.

Use Yourself Up.

This morning I was sitting down in my makeshift office, the living room of this old farmhouse in which I'm living for the winter. And because it was still dark and gloomy out, the sun just barely awake, I reached for a candle to light. But then I hesitated, the way we feel the need to save nice things for a different time that might never come, so then I didn't light it. Despite what I'm learning that it's not the things it's the people, like the car crash I saw on the road, the car flipped over and the car still there, but the people, the people were gone. And which do you think mattered more to the loved ones? The person or the thing? Why do we hoard these things when it's the life that matters? We can't take things with us, only the love we've given and received.

Then I reached for an old fragile book, but stopped again, the way we do with special old things so they don't get even more used, saving those too. Not savoring them— but saving them. And I think of people who survive disasters, and it wasn't the things that mattered, it was them, their loved ones that mattered. When faced with imminent doom, no- thing matters but life itself. And then I got a message from the things themselves: "Use me," the things urged. "Being used gives us life, being used makes us comes alive."

It's the same way with us, I thought. You have to "use" yourself. Not hoard yourself, your energy, your creativity, your love, Expend the energy to receive the energy. Don't waste yourself by "saving" yourself. Use yourself up by going, giving, doing, loving. Your energy and horizon will expand, expand, expand. I think how much you are living is in direct proportion to how much you are giving.

Since I left the rescue farm on the Vineyard I lived on last summer I haven't felt so deliciously used up the way I love to be. I haven't felt used the way a day of action with the animals sucked me dry of all my self-invented fear. Every day I was up at dawn, stepping out of bed into a warm pile of Labradors we boarded, making coffee and filling their bowls. I had to keep the restless dogs in the cabin before I let the chickens out of their den in the backyard, then I released the dogs in a euphoric stampede, then I fed the horses, the turkeys, the chickens, the peacocks and the rabbit. And I remember how much I loved it, how good I was at it, despite my sarcastic protests about being a bonafide "animal waitress." Because I was getting used up by all those needy animals all day long, and the more I gave, the more I cup-runneth-over got.

The things in our lives, the time we have, all say "use us up and see, watch how the magical kitchen of your heart only makes more energy, more love to give. A loving, giving soul feels how our bodies feel after being used for exercise, when the energy we've spent only awakens us to more energy—a greater, cleaner more buzzing energy. We are made of endless energy light and love. We are infinite. To get more, give more. To be of service, let go and align yourself with your source. Empty it all out and offer yourself to the Universe, let it fill you up with the good stuff it's so longing to give you. Give more to live more. Giving is living. The more you are giving the more you are living. Use yourself up.

[That thing you're resisting: Dive In.

"Can we make a deal," she said, "Not to run when things get real."]

Winter, 2011. Free Union Virginia

No More Tantrums.

I don't have anything to say today except that life happens when you let go. Life is so lovely and when you finally stop throwing a tantrum like a toddler who's not getting her way with Mother Universe, when you finally stop pointing fingers. When you realize everything you're complaining about, you could change.

When you finally stop making choices from the ego because you finally see again they are getting you nowhere—you only made a few, because maybe the universe wasn't looking, or maybe she would cut you a break and understand because everything seemed so hard, but this life is not a bargain, and you were watching, YOU saw yourself do it. There's no day off from Love. And everything is between you and God and the angels, doesn't life always feel like "Smile, You're on God's Camera?" And haven't you noticed there is no "Getting Away" With Anything? And then you start making the right choices from your soul again and life moves back into flow again. And it's not rocket science. It's doing the work, because doing the work works. When you take care of your life, life takes care of you.

So, exhausted, angry, in the throes of despair you finally give in like a tired child who feels a million years old and you fall down into your life, you give up, belly up, surrender. And then it rises to comfort you, it welcomes you home. Your life welcomes you back into it. And then the riches rise up from that earth you were stomping all over in vain, your were spinning out to find your fruitless destination, when it was all underfoot. You just couldn't see it because you refused to, because you were holding on so tightly to your demands of what your life should be and who should be in it and how they should be and who you should be. Patiently, a better and abundant reality waited in the wings of your hysterics.

I walked into a field of horses yesterday, five female polo horses had been left behind when their owners went to Florida for the winter. My roommate Barbara was care taking them, sometimes she takes me along to feed them as the sun rises and sets. Two looked like chocolate-colored, lanky overgrown deer, with big brown eyes and long lashes, splashes of white paint on their noses. Then there was one who looked just like Eloise, she had red hair and a messy mohawk adorned with spiky green burs, a squat muscular body and a sincerely inquisitive wide face, with those long red Kardashian eye lashes. The sun was going down over the farm, sherbet pinks and yellows fell over the Virginia farmland, and across the hill a man rode his lawn mower around pine trees he'd wrapped in colored Christmas lights. The horses slowly started to circle me, and one of the brown girls hooked her lanky neck on my shoulder, her heavy head resting on my back. Then two of them started to sniff me up and down, while one licked my hand really softly. We stood there for fifteen minutes, I hummed a bit while ancient reiki symbols floated through me. There was no wind; it was so still. With a bit of goopy orange sun left in the sky, I ran the mile home from the barn and took a hot shower.

Then I got in bed with Gracie, into the borrowed bed at this farmhouse but under my own comforter, the one Amy bought me after my fiancé left me and I left California alone. She bought it to remind me of the ocean—our house had been at the shore of Santa Monica. In the mornings on the walks with the dogs, I always walked where I could see the water, but I never let myself actually get in. It was a lot like what I do with life, a lot like the distance I keep, the glass between me and what some call living. What some call a real life. The comforter is a soft, washed-out blue with coral and pink conch shells and green tangles of seaweed. When I moved into that temporary basement apartment in Brooklyn, when I had no idea where to go after he left me, she sent it to cover me in my empty bed. Whenever I pull it up over my shoulders at night, I think of Amy and her undying love for my sister and me, her late sister's children. And I think about the kind of love that never leaves, no matter how rough the seas.

["*Shh*, be quiet. I am showing you the way.

You're not lost, you are just shouting over

the directions." —Your Heart]

[Winter's Patience: Do you have the patience Winter requires of you/ To let things die/ Before they can be born anew?]

Winter, 2011. Free Union, Virginia

Stay:

When mom was in remission she flew us to California. She knew she was really really sick, sicker than we knew she was. Maybe my sister did but I preferred denial. I preferred that glass between me and the reality. We were living the high life out there, a bed and breakfast in Pt. Reyes at the top of a rose bush covered hill, you could sit in the hot tub and see the ocean. We rented a Mustang convertible to drive down Rte 1, from Big Sur. I was a testy fifteen year old, sullen, confused, torn open about every little thing, except, of course, every bone in my body resisted the truth of my mother's sickness. I threw all my walls up against it. I played the sullen teenager till her very end, as if in defiance of life itself, for doing this to her, to us. Angry. My ravenous thirst for "normalcy" had begun with my parents divorce when we were eleven, and it grew insatiable when the cancer diagnosis came when we were twelve. I railed against these violent disruptions as if by resisting them they wouldn't be happening. On the drive down the coast the top was down, mom in her cashmere and fragile gold jewelry at the wheel, my sister in front, me in back, and the night fell inky black, fierce white stars puncturing the black air of night, they were so close and twinkling, like we could reach through the chilly whooshing air and touch them. Beneath us the surf crashed, you couldn't see it but you could feel it and hear it, and far off to the right you could see the silky white milk of the moon spilling on the sea's horizon. And I realized Mom started to go slower and slower and slower, and at first I was annoyed and angry because I was so insecure & self conscious and she was holding up all these cars behind us who wanted to go faster, they began to stack up in a long herd behind us, they impatiently flashed their lights at us to speed up or pull over. But she wouldn't speed up, she just sailed slowly around the curves, Eric Clapton Unplugged in the cd player, and every time I hear a track from that record I'm back in that car. Finally after I pleaded with her, she pulled over to let the cars pass, and a few people actually clapped at her as they passed us, then thy flew fast down the highway. I cringed but Mom laughed, her high golden laugh. And with no one behind us, she crept back onto the highway into that fresh California night air, and we just kept sailing slowly down the highway, until I realized she was savoring it , lingering in it, feeling it, memorizing it, being alive with it. And then we were all present. And when you're present, that's when you make it last forever. And that's what I've been doing the past few days, like I stepped back into my present life like a portal. And I am remembering the great grace of my mother who knew she didn't have as much time as everyone thought, and so she slowed her life down, and she made sure she'd remember it. She reached out and touched it. Because less than a year later she'd made all the memories in her lifetime that she ever would, there would be no more making memories with mom after that. So she went slowly, slowly, slowly. And you, please, slowly, slowly, slowly, walk through your life and touch it all and be touched by it all. And embrace and an imprint it into your heart. Because it all changes, just like that. Slowly, slowly, slowly. Don't rush. Stay here.

["I am learning," she said, "to savor my existence."]

Winter, 2011. Free Union, Virginia.

Earthing.

When I am spinning out of control and losing my sense of place and self, I like to put my bare feet in the grass and dig them deep into earth's carpet. [I traded the red carpet for the green]. I am taken back to the present, my place in the nature of things, the temporary state of this moment, the cycle of life and death, my feet digging into the very soil in which my body will rest forever when my soul moves on. Yes indeed, this moment will pass, the drama is all a dream, and yes indeed, you are safe.

I was having my coffee on the porch as the white gold morning sun fell on the yard and I asked myself, "How come I got to wake up to another day?" There are many, many souls who did not wake up in a healthy body today, or who did not wake up at all, did not get another day here on earth. Many people much kinder, more patient, more loving, less caught up in the dark, didn't get to wake up today. But I got to step outside and feel the warmth of the winter sun on my face and the gentle wind in my hair, and I got to see the drips of water on Gracie's whiskers and I took a big clean gulp of breath. I am never guaranteed another day. I am only ever guaranteed the moment. Not the next one.

Our time feels like it's rushing by faster than the wind, nothing to stop it but the golden net of love, the only thing we can take with us, what we gave, and life feels charged with a greater urgency to answer those calls from places inside us so deep we can't fathom, voices that seem to speak from the stars themselves, from the far corners of infinity. Voices that know us better than we ever will. Sometimes I feel like I am one of those Russian dolls, you open one painted wooden shell and there is another doll, then you open that shell and there is another, and it is endless. One shell is cracked open and a new me rises. I grow and harden into the new version, and then that form is cracked open to reveal yet another new me. As one wall is broken down and a new one appears. I am shedding my skin fast, and I am no longer afraid of this process. I am not holding onto my old life anymore, how can I when it changes so fast. So I allow the new.

I am asked to look forward and to heal my wounds so that I can awaken fully into abundance, service, and love and the expansiveness that calls and awaits. I am asked to constantly expand my horizon and un-learn the old ways that no longer work. Drop the weeds that no longer serve me. Push the old dreams out of the boat and sail lighter.

That I am still here is no accident, that we each woke up again today is no accident. Even an "accident" is not an accident. There are paths to explore and walls to break down and fears to face and new ways to love and to live. We are deepening into the mystery more than ever. I am not moving into this new time alone. It is my intention to expand into every cell of my being, to align with Source and to merge with my highest self, and to live the questions with a voracious appetite and unshakable faith.

Happy Holidays, the Present is your greatest present.

[The ego holds on, and Love Lets go. Something Beautiful is trying to happen if you just let go.]

Winter, 2011. Free Union, Virginia

Book a One-Way Flight.

Two days before 2012 and I'm feeling like the Internet is as bad as the television, just the sleeker, more sophisticated version of a deathly portal, sucking years out of your life. During your time on the Internet, you are not breathing consciously, touching anyone's skin, looking in anyone's eyes, holding your open soul to theirs, helping anyone up, holding someone or something close, taking in a view, using your body, praying, meditating, feeling the wind, evolving…you know, living. And so I hear, turn it off, it's killing you. Run.

But then I think, if you have to use it one more time, use it to book yourself a one-way flight to Hawaii or Peru or Costa Rica of that place you've dreamed of going since you were a child but everyone told you you should wait to go with someone or just… wait. For a better time. That never comes.

So book your ticket now. Don't wait. You will know when it is time to come back, but you do not know now. You know nothing now. And that's a good way to live. Empty handed in the mystery. Board the plane in just a beautiful flowing caftan, with only your mala in hand. Meditate the entire flight. "May all beings know peace, may all beings be free from suffering. May all beings know peace, may all beings be free from suffering. May all beings know peace, may all beings be free from suffering." Envision leaving the old life behind, walking through the white light door to your new life of love and service. All you can see is light, and the old suffering and the tiny self all just falls away, like a crumbling cliff into the sea.

Get there. Strip, stretch to the sky, feet sinking in clean white sand, then jump in the cold blue water. Become alive. Wet, slick, goose bumped. Weightless. Float. Feel lifted, safe, cared for on the waves. Know this is how you walk through life when you have faith. Do naked yoga on the beach, reunite with your soul in the rain forest, where she has been waiting, chanting for you, in lotus. Now awakened and aligned, fully become your life's purpose, fully become love. Touch everyone with your love until it spreads over the earth like a golden blanket. Touch everyone with love until mother earth rains tears of love and love rules the world. Get loved so deep and hard your own bones feels crushed back into mother earth, where they belong. Love, make love, birth love, then when you are done, float into the cosmos, become a star, shine down love forever, with the same energy that glows in your soul right now. Shine down from a sea of love in which you are never, ever alone, and in which your existence reminds others of the same truth, that no one is ever, ever alone, that security is an illusion and the only time we really have is now, our time is fleeting faster than that sinking sun over the horizon. (Remember that time you thought your whole life was ending, when really it was just the beginning?)

[ALL KINDS OF WEATHER. Upon re-rising on the earth/ the Goddess looked around, shook her head and said/ "wait- let me get this straight/ the Only place women are allowed to be 'bad' is bed/ otherwise they must always act/ like good little girls?/ Well that isn't true and it just won't do/ Don't they realize women are all kinds of weather/ and every imaginable color of / feather?/ Like animals too long caged/ Their souls are in a rage/ I've reawoken in their hearts/ and now I'm moving through their hands/ it won't be long now until their/ song/ is heard throughout the land."]

Winter, 2011. Free Union, Virginia

I Wish She Had Danced More.

Fifteen years ago today my mother died, less than a month after my sister and I had turned seventeen. We walked out of the hospital into the night under heavy snow, falling like globs of cake batter from the very quiet, dark sky. We didn't want to go home to the empty house, her empty bed, so that night we ate dinner on the downtown mall with our older cousins, so cool they had never really had time for us until now. We sat in a dimly-lit French restaurant draped with reds and golds, and we picked at plates of pasta and sipped wine from the older girls' glasses. The girls had lost their father, my mother's brother, a few years earlier than us. We were numb and exhausted and our cheeks were soaked and spongy by the time we asked for the check, but the chef had overheard our news and he had comped the meal. "I'm sorry," someone had written on the bill.

And, "I'm sorry," our waiter had shouted as we left and pushed out into the night. We walked through the streets holding on to each other in the thick winter jackets thrown over our shoulders by adults in the hospital room. On our way home to the motherless house the sky moaned, and lightning cracked through the snow, electrifying the clouds. You had to stop to look up, in awe and overwhelmed by the magnitude of the day. It looked like the lights were flickering on and off in heaven. Tiny beneath the heavens, you had to toss your head back to look up at the dramatic display, your breath in the air, for a moment, afraid of nothing, the worst had happened and blood still ran through your veins and breath still filled your lungs and that was all you knew. It was a fitting goodnight for a woman who didn't go gently into the night.

It is hard, on a day like today not to feel grateful to be here. It's hard because I watched her fight so hard to stay here, I watched her be pulled to the other side as her hand went limp in mine, her last breath taken. Not a day, and rarely an hour, goes by I don't think of her, and parts of her live on in me. Your loved ones will do the same for you. We are beings of Love. We are here to see what our love can create. We are here to see what our love can overcome, and how far it can reach. I woke up and wore her blue silk Japanese bathrobe, and turned on the music she loved. Then I went to the farm and stood in the morning mist as the horses circled around me. They took turns laying their heavy heads on my shoulder, showing me more affection than usual. I came home and my best friend had written that she was listening to Bob Seger in honor of my mom, who liked to dance, often barefoot in white jeans and a t-shirt to Bob Seger and The Band. My best friend never "met" mom, but she knows her through me. They have a lot of geeky and wonderful things in common. So maybe you can do the same, if you'd like, or you can go listen to or do something you love. Either way if we all gave ourselves up with abandon to something or someone we love today, I think that would be a wonderful way to express gratitude for our time here. Absolutely throw yourself at the feet of Love. It doesn't hurt, in the morning, to walk out first thing, and shout "thank you," to the everything and the endlessness that is always and forever listening, waiting to hear your sweet song.

[i wish she had let herself be a little bit more wild. i wish she had let herself dance barefoot a whole lot more. i wish she could have laughed and shaken it off more. i wish she had loved herself with abandon in the face of any rejection. I wish she trusted herself, and heard her own voice and used it more. i wish she hadn't put off what she dreamed of, that she had held each moment of her life like a blade of grass and drowned out all the noise that told her to be anyone but her sweet endless self. i wish she could have known that nothing but her happiness mattered and she was loved bigger than she could have ever imagined. i wish she could have tossed herself screaming into the ocean more, and blissfully into her own love for herself more. and i wish, i had wish i had told her i loved her, constantly, like a song i could never stop singing. and that i hadn't just said it but that I had shown her shown her shown her.]

Oh my God, how you are loved. Oh my God, how you are wanted. Oh my God, how you are needed. Oh my God, how you belong. Oh my God, can't you hear, right now, the angels sing your song.

Winter, 2011. Free Union, Virginia.

Formerly Agnostic.

My father, as far as I know, is an agnostic, which is what I was for the better part of my life. Talking with him after my spiritual awakening can be difficult and awkward, broken up with strange looks and silences. I remember at the beginning of the journey, being in the Kripalu bookstore just voraciously sucking up the wisdom of the titles, and a woman with a thick Massachusetts accent said of her awakening, "No one tells you, you find yourself, you lose your husband." You gain a lot. You lose a lot. It is, as everything, a double-edged sword.

Yesterday, because my stepmother is in Europe, I spent a full day alone with him. I haven't done this in a year, since he came to see me on Martha's Vineyard and we had a blizzard, a month before my awakening. I love my father so much. So dearly. The distance I've felt with him of late has been a great pain to me. Being fully present during my time with him can be, as real life is, heart-in-a-vice hard at times but also very rewarding. In the morning in the kitchen I told him how I've been thinking of buying a ticket to Hawaii, how I read Hank Wesselman's book "The Bowl of Light" and now I'm drawn to the spirit of Pele, the Goddess of Fire who rules over the Big Island.

I want to go for nine nights, and I'll go alone. I told Dad how I want to take a workshop about—

"Self help?" Dad asked, shaking his head. "That stuff's all the same…"

"No, Dad, I've told you. Self-love. A way of life. Forgiveness, self-forgiveness, compassion…" He was gone again.

When he came back later he moved the conversation to me getting a steady job and settling down in one place. This is an ongoing conversation as I am unable, at this point in my life, to explain to my father that I no longer seek any "normal" or pre-paved path. [This from me who, for the first 30 years of my life, only wished to be "normal."] He is nervous for me. I can totally understand this. I have completely left the shore. I can barely remember what it was like to be on the shore. Instead of trying to tame them, I have dived headfirst into these utterly mysterious unknown waters of my heart. He is nervous. So am I, sometimes. Not today.

The morning bumped along like that, but I continued to show up and be patient with him. In the evening there was an unspoken, gentle truce—we ran errands, went running on the dark suburban streets with the dogs and came home to make pizza and drink our non-alcoholic beer in front of Chevy Chase's "Christmas Vacation."

Before dinner I came up from the basement, I was finished packing for the farmhouse, and Dad was out in the driveway on his fancy new grill.

"Can I help?" I called from the back door.

"That's okay," my Dad said, laying out slices of green pepper on the pizza dough. "I'll do this." He crossed his arms over the grill apron he wears, the one that has pockets for his cooking timer and tongs.

And then he said, his back to me, "Why don't you go square away that ticket to Hawaii. You want to make sure you get a good price on that flight."

It's high time for me to fly. I've been too afraid to fly since my fiancé put me on that plane, two weeks before our would-be wedding, and said goodbye forever. It's time to grow my wings again. The day I broke up with normal was the first day of my magical life.

[I am a wild feminine animal/ I survive on my natural instinct/ If it feels right It is right/ If it feels wrong/ It is wrong/ I let my inner Goddess guide me/ and Love moves me along. She said, "I had to be true to myself. It was the only way to survive."]

Winter, 2012, The Big Island Hawaii.

Meeting Pele.

My first day in Hawaii I rose and immediately walked toward the paved road toward the ocean. A few cars passed on the mile and a half walk, offering rides, I waved them on. But halfway there an old woman in white stopped, and I got in. She said her name was Rainbow, she drove an old green car that smelled of cigarette smoke, and five minutes later she let me out at the beach path with barely a word. I made my way down the jagged path and despite the towering size of the waves, and the "oohs" and "aws" at their sheer massiveness from people on the beach, I just walked, dream-like into the water. It all happened so fast, like a blink, from rising in my cabin room to sleep walking into the water.

Looking back it reminds me of Virginia Woolf, walking into the water for her final swim with stones in her pockets, I had my own weights of attachments to the past, pulling me, making me heavy, my head so thick with memories, you know, who we walk when we're not present.

And then, almost immediately, I got sucked in a deadly rip tide. My arms went limp like noodles, all the strength drained, like being pulled down into the ocean's great drain. I couldn't keep my head above the waves. I was sputtering up through the water. I was in a powerful, churning whirlpool and when I surfaced, gasping, I was pushed against an enormous slippery black craggly rock, the size of a wall, and I was stuck in a pocket of water that wouldn't release me, clutching me, grasping me, pulling me under with relentless watery hands.

"This is it," I thought. "This is how it's going to happen to me." I looked around frantically for help, and there was someone else in the water. A man, who was watching me, he had deeply tanned skin, a shock of gray hair and the most piercing blue eyes, like the ocean on a much calmer day than this one.

"Help," I cried, "I need help."

He nodded, serious, but so calm. I could only see those blue eyes coming toward me, through the slushing water, staring into mine, keeping the connection like a lifeline.

"I'm coming," he said, "I'm coming. You need to breathe. Breathe."

But I couldn't, I had started to swallow the sea instead of air. Then William slipped his arms around my waist and he swam me to shore, I let go in his arms, I was held, I can still feel his bare arm around my bare waist in the water.

"You're alright," he said, "You're fine now," he said, as we reached the craggy shore where a beautiful half naked woman with long shiny black hair breastfed her child. And without words he left me in her arms in the black sand and he returned to that water. Serenely, she held me in one arm and her child in the other, and the child was calm even through my shaking and crying.

When I could speak, I discovered her name was Jade and his name was William. Jade was a Kundalini teacher in New York before the Big Island called her, William was a Tibetan monk before his spirit was called home to to the Big Island as well. The breastfeeding child was theirs.

They told me about Pele, by whom the Big Island is spiritually governed. She's a fiery, passionate, transformative goddess named Pele. She doesn't take well to people sleep walking through life, no she's a fire-walker. She's Passion Herself. She is the destroyer as well as the creator. She will kill what needs to be killed in order to create the new. She is not for the faint or weak of heart. That beach, Kehena Beach, translates to Black Death Beach. They say that beach will either take your life or change it. Jade never goes in, she knows its power. William, clearly, is not afraid. Thank God. I mean, thank Goddess.

"The energy changed, it darkened, as soon as you went in the water," Jade told me as the four of us drove away in their van, William had one hand, which was wrapped in a blood red mala, on the wheel, his eyes still watched me in the rear view mirror. "Brave and stupid walk a thin line," he said. He wasn't big on words. He said actions spoke what one needed to say.

"You were always going to be ok," said William. "I knew to watch you, I knew as soon as you walked in," he said. "God told me," he said, "to watch you in the water."

"Pele needed your breath as an offering," they agreed.

As soon as they said that I remembered how I felt in the water, I felt the questions of the earth and the sea, like great ancient rumblings.

"Do you really want to live? Do you really want to be here?" the water asked in a deep ancient voice, in a language that asked my soul its one true question. "Do you want to be here? Are you really here? Do you want your old life or do you want this life?"

To choose the old life is to choose death.

Make a choice.

"She put you through the rinse cycle," Jade said as we sipped on fresh coconuts at an open air market and bought five dollar dresses, having skipped past small talk and become intimate friends after William saved my life.

Thank you Pele, it was a violent baptism, and a shocking rebirth, and it was exactly what I needed.

I wasn't supposed to die that day, I was supposed to once and for all Live, to answer the Call to Live this Life Now. And I was supposed to be saved by a Tibetan monk and a Kundalini teacher, because that is how all of this has happened, my Personal Awakening. I was saved by words of Truth and Compassion, and saved by my Kundalini, that serpent of feminine energy that rose up my spine and shattered me awake. And, I found out later that Hawaiian legend says that Pele often appears as an old woman in white.

[You say you love mysteries well now's your chance to prove it / With an open heart and total trust bow to it/ Kneel at the throne of the unknown/ Stop demanding to know /Take the present's hand and let go/ Surrender the tiny ego to the unlimited ocean of soul/ Forget what you think feel how you feel /Savor every moment like its your last meal.]

Winter, 2012, The Big Island

Kalani.

On the lush green lawn outside of my room in Hawaii there was a statue of a woman I had never seen before, a stone woman holding a vase of water with the most serene look on her face, like inside she was swimming in the stars, swimming in the Universe, and she was ecstatic and she was eternally, endlessly, blissfully pleased. Serenity is not a word I was even conscious of until last year, but it has begun to sink into my being in my most aligned hours. It is yummy, it is like honey. It feels gooey, it feels like our destiny. I was called again and again to this woman's feet, for just a taste of her inner bliss. What is inside is outside. Love on the inside breeds love on the outside. Calm on the inside breeds calm on the outside. For the first three days I cried, and would sit in front of her with an offering everyday, flowers, my mother's broken rosary, chocolate. Through my tears, I would look at her, and she would just smile, in total peace, because she knew the dark is just a bridge to the light, and that it passes, and that peace and love is what we find on the other side. On the third day I knelt before her, a woman from my group (also a Kundalini teacher) walked up beside me, and placed her hand on my back- that's when the release started, and the shift started.

If we don't allow our walls to crack, where will the light come in? How will it find us?

Holly's touch brought a flood of relief. I rose to head to class, when my newly found intuition said, "don't rush, and don't walk to the left, walk to the right." I turned right, and a furry figure moving in the jungle grass caught my eye. I walked over to find a puppy the size of a bunny, and we played on all fours until she lead me to her mother, a Shamanic medicine woman sitting in the hot tub.

"Oh," I said to Lynda, "I think I've been looking for you." I was too late for class at that point, and I knew my leader would understand, I was tired of bringing my funky energy into the group. I settled down into the hot tub with the woman.

"I've been having such a hard time with Pele," I confessed. "Should I be afraid of her? Are you?"

"Oh no," laughed Lynda. "I love that Woman. I WORSHIP her."

I was quiet.

"I think she tried to drown me the other day."

Lynda said "Oh that current goes straight to Tahiti, you would have been there in 3 months."

"That's not my preferred method of travel," I told her.

"Have you tried talking to her? Clearly she's trying to talk to you."

I hadn't. "How do I do it? Will you help me?"

"Yes Honey, but whatever works for you. Whatever your Ritual is. Honoring is Honoring."

Still, Lynda and I rose out of the hot tub in search of the right leaves and sea salt, and I performed my first ritual that left me glowing, aligned and smiling, it cleared the energy in the room, it allowed space for Presence. It created an environment of trust and peace.

The next morning and every morning and night after that I sat at the stone goddess's feet. I would tell her how locked inside I felt, I would ask her for compassion and strength, how I was looking for me. I told her I wasn't strong, but I wanted to be.

When I came home I read more about her, her name is Kwan Yin, the Chinese Buddhist Goddess of Compassion, the Goddess of Mercy. Her name means "she who harkens to the cries of the world." She's also said to save the drowning- is it possible Pele pulled me under and Kwan Yin saved me? To show me two of the many faces of the goddess, of woman? Both Fierce and Compassionate? Who better to die to than Pele and who better to cry to than Kwan Yin?

Honoring is Honoring.

When Lynda was getting in her car she yelled out, "Honey!!"

I turned back.

"Tears aren't always bad, you know."

"You're right," I shouted, "They say the cure for anything is salt water - sweat, tears, or the sea." [Isak Dinesen said that. And didn't I have all three in Hawaii?]

"I like that," she smiled.

And then she was gone.

[He said, "You're the kind of woman, I think of when the moon is full, and you're the kind of woman, who makes me realize, I've been such a fool."]

Winter, 2012. The Big Island, Hawaii.

It Has to Work Now.

I was in the backseat of a car in Hawaii, four of us women driving through a tropical rainstorm, all talking about love and relationships. A woman can meet another woman for the first time, and a moment later be sharing her deepest secrets and desires. When we are not afraid of intimacy, of being seen or getting rejected, we are privy to powerful and deep connections that make us feel real, human. I do this with other women all the time, we recognize each other in airports, in gas stations. I often remember, as a child, waiting for my mother in a lingering car outside of a restaurant or gas station, getting impatient, and then going in to see her holding a sobbing woman behind a counter, while shooting me that "go wait in the car" look. Every encounter started with a simple "hi." My journey is your journey, your journey is mine. I feel what you are feeling. I hear what you are saying. Our stories connect us.

The woman next to me in the backseat started to talk about her problems with the man in her life, he had disappeared again because he wasn't getting his way. He wanted all these things, he had all these rules, really, for how it had to work, if it was even going to, and she was deeply attached to their past, how they could have done things differently, and their future, how they could do things differently, and they were stuck in that awful place of Love's Limbo. I remembered being in that place myself for years, and I felt the hopelessness of this situation, a sneaking, "I don't think love should be so hard," whisper but I didn't say anything. By the way, not saying anything felt really good. Just witnessing it letting it flow, without your control, keeping your mouth shut and your mind open, when you're not sure of what to say. Allowing the situation to be what it is, not manipulating it for your own comfort is a secret I'm just discovering.

Anyway who was I to tell her heart what to do. Love is why we are here, love is the great eternal mystery, so we end up doing some pretty wild and foolish things in its name. Well, if we're really living, I think. I would rather be a fool for love than a fool for fear.

From the front seat, a beautiful, wise yogini mother in a successful 25+ year relationship spoke up. It felt like her place to talk, as the group's elder.

She was shaking her head. "It has to work now," she said. "If it is not working now, it's not going to work later."

And then I thought Yes, if you don't love your life now, you don't love your life. Now is all there is. It has to work now. You have to love it now. What does tomorrow have that today doesn't?

BOOM. The car was quiet.

Then I opened my mouth. "Oh my God, I wish you were there to tell me that years ago," I said.

You have got to get out of the trunk and get back at the wheel. You have got to drive your own life. To change your future, change your present. Be the person now that you hope to be one day, be the woman of your dreams, today, right now. Be Her Now. If you can dream her you can be her. Like the flick of a switch, Turn Her On.

[She said it so matter of factly, just like the trees have roots and the sky is blue, she said, "until you truly believe you're lovable, you're never going to let anyone, truly love you."]

Winter, 2012, The Big Island.

My friend Sylvie.

My friend Sylvie from the Hawaii retreat was scuba diving in the depths of the ocean in Bali when one of the ancient sages of the ocean, a sea turtle, bypassed her husband and swam right up to her. Small blond Sylvie, a mystic healer sage of a woman, watched the turtle approach her, slowly, gracefully, purposefully, and then its head stopped right at her heart, right at that heart chakra. In her divinely Shamanic way, Sylvie knew it was time to ask the turtle for wisdom. She said all animals have wisdom for us if we are humble enough to ask.

"And then he spoke," she told me in her rich French accent by the pool in Hawaii, as dusk's first breeze came through the trees. He said, "Love is not a feeling, it is a state. Be in love at all times. When you are in love you are in the present. When you are in the present, you are in all times."

Another time Sylvie was scuba diving beneath the surface of the ocean, in that watery heaven, where all you can see when you look up is light, and all you can hear is the rhythm of your breath and the pounding of your heart, just like when you were in the womb, and everyone and everything is either floating or flying around you. And a turtle also stopped in her presence, and, again, stopped to talk to her heart, right there, once more. [Shouldn't we all just be talking to each other's hearts? Heart to Heart? Is there any other way to talk? The ancient wise creature is telling us, this is how you speak to another being, you speak at heart-level.] Sylvie waited for the wisdom. "Don't look at me," said the wise old creature. "You should be looking at your own heart."

[She asked me why

I wanted to fit in

when the ones who stand out

are the ones who change the world.]

Late Winter, 2012 Free Union, Virginia

Building Back From the Smashes.

I heard a fable about us humans that at the beginning of time each of our souls was smashed and scattered into tiny pieces- flung far and wide into the cosmos. That's why some of us, those who dare, spend our lives searching for our true selves and slowly but magnificently piece ourselves back together. Doesn't it feel just like a great big mystery adventure you're living, like Indiana Jones, or Romancing the Stone? Sometimes you're so close to the treasure, sometimes you're even clutching it on the top of a mountain, singing your song, and sometimes you're in the dark, in a cave, waiting out the night? Isn't it just as thrilling and exhilarating as any Hollywood epic? Could there be any greater adventure than finding yourself and your highest calling? Your true purpose? Your soul chose to be here! You wanted in! You bought a ticket! You are on the ride of your life! It's happening right now! Not later or yesterday or in half a year, now. If your life feels like it's on hold, be bold. Make a move toward what moves you.

[To find your true love /You've got to find your true you.]

Late Winter, 2011. Free Union, Virginia

Hearts Like Pillows.

My friend Joanna and I took a class on human anatomy this summer at Kripalu, and we discovered that as fetuses in the womb, the head rests on the heart in the early stages. When we were tiny little creatures we slept on them like pillows, like boom boom boom beating pillows. We were born listening to our hearts. Somewhere along the way we forgot, it got too scary, it asked too much, it felt too vulnerable, it hurt. Now, for me, to listen to both the heart's steady, solid beats as well as its whispered messages is my return There is a rhythm to life and there is a path being whispered, and it's all inside of you. The rhythm of the heart is the one to move to, to dance to in life.

Last January I was alone in the cabin during a winter storm. It was a very peaceful time of tea and jigsaw puzzles and writing and handmade pizza from scratch. One morning while I was doing the dishes a fat red cardinal visited me outside of the window, proud and puffy, and he would come back for a few days after that. [I loved that windowsill, full like an altar, of candles and angels and seashells]. The shock of his red coat, the color of blood and love against the pure white snow was so beautiful that I looked up his symbolism. I called my aunt Amy and read it to her, and it was something like, "The sight of the red cardinal reminds us that even in winter, love and warmth is always near. The cardinal reminds us to stay proud, stay strong in the cold wind and is a symbol of warmth in hard times. It can also mean that you will know love sooner than you think." No matter what, love is never far. Love is right here. Even if you don't feel it right then, even if you can't see it. Especially then.

My friend Jen married this solid and smart guy, named Scott. [She met him in English class, take note]. He's great with all of us girls and is always the formidable "trooper." He often has the job of everyone's date by the end of the night when he becomes a walking hat rack of our coats and bags. He's always buying his wife's friends their drinks or helping them find a cab, all the while being a shoulder to lean on. He and Jen are a great pair, she'll send him out to the dance floor when she sees another friend swaying alone— and he'll oblige, even act like it was his idea. That part to me, that reveals his true character. A gentle, man. This December when my friend got married in New York, he walked a gaggle of us to the after party. At the bar I leaned on him, weary, it was far past my bedtime. We got to talking about romantic love, and I told him I was waving the white flag for a while. With Jen rested her head sleepily on his other shoulder, he said: "They all wrong until the One that's Right. Love is impossible for everyone until the moment that it happens."

[She saw me sleeping

beneath blankets of shame and fear

and she said, "Oh No No My Dear,

Get Up Shake it Off.

If you are waiting till you have it all together

You will be waiting forever

And one day you will lie down and you will never move again

So Dry your eyes and Rise Rise

Move. While. You. Still. Can."]

Late Winter, 2012, Free Union, Virginia

Once Upon a Time.

Once upon a time there was a little girl, like a lot of little girls, with big dreams and a big heart and lots of potential. One day her mother got really, really sick and a few years later the little girl watched her die in a sterile hospital room. Broken-hearted, angry, and afraid, the little girl started a lifetime of running from the black, dark river of death. Her heart never healed, and she went crashing through life without a map, brakes, or a helmet, getting out of one burning car only to get into another. On the side of the road lay all the men, towns, and dream jobs she burned through. She eventually found a woman with long black hair and no life behind her eyes to give her pills that made her sleep through her days like her nights, slack-jawed, sedated, with shallow breaths. Then her mother's eldest sister, her beloved Aunt, whose words had been like pinpricks of light through the black veil the girl lived under, died too. And the girl's heart, already half-dead, smashed to pieces.

There was still her mother's younger sister, but the girl had stopped reaching out to family. She was too tired. She was too ashamed. Then her musician lover, her last lifeline to the world, gave up and left her. After all that time he called off the wedding and sent her long white satin wedding dress back himself, then he went on tour and sang songs about the death of their love in dark clubs to faceless people. She would sleep for another year, and that whole year she just wished someone could cut her heart out and bury it, she kept dreaming of a witch doctor healing her, but none appeared, so she took the pills, she drank the wine. Finally, there was nowhere left to run, all the bridges were burned and there were no trap doors left, and so the loneliest girl in the world dropped to her knees in a cabin on a magical Island and asked for help.

"Are you out there, is anyone there?" she asked. "I know this is no life. Have I ruined every chance? Please," she said, "Either help me to die, or help me to live. I cannot take another step on this path."

It took a few moments, but the girl stayed on her knees. Something was happening, something was coming. Then Presence filled the room. "I see you. I see you. I've seen you all along," it hummed. There was a glowing finger of light on her heart, it felt just like if I were to touch your heart right now. Her good-as-dead heart throbbed red, awoken, sore from years of sleep.

"It hurts," she told the Presence, grasping at her chest.

"Good,"said Presence, rejoicing. "That means it's working, it's turned back on," It said. "It's opening now." Open like a dam that would never, ever close again. The light was unstoppable now. Clutching at her heart, she gasped. So much release. So much sensation. So much expansion. So much Love. "Oh my God," she said.

"You have to feel your pain to feel your joy," said Presence. "Without pain you cannot know joy. You have to touch your wounds to heal them. Without dark you cannot know light. Without sleeping you cannot know what it is to awake." It said.

Every thing she looked at made her cry, every thing was so beautiful she had to cry and laugh at the miracle of all of it. Was this what it felt like to be alive? She felt her first tears and her first laughs. Her hands in the air, opening and closing, the sense of touch returned, everything felt miraculous, sensual. She saw everything as alive, made of dancing matter, dancing life. The air sparkled with gold flecks the way it had when she as a child, before she had grown bitter and dead inside. Everything she looked at, everything in the natural world she could now see it for what it was, a masterpiece, a miracle. Her beating heart, that had beat by itself all these years without her, now banged inside her chest like the powerful pounding of ancient Shaman's drum. The feel of her breath filling her lungs, they felt like her first breaths, the breaths of someone who had almost drowned for good, only to take in air again. She sucked the rich magic air in greedily. Her steps, they felt like the powerful, victorious first steps of an infant learning to walk. She even wobbled a bit as she crossed the floor, and she put such conscious intention into each movement. She wanted to feel every little thing, and she knew she was part of every little thing. Where she once felt dead and disconnected to all, now every single cell had been electrified and re-connected, plugged back into some great, universal auspicious socket. Her entire body trembled awake. She could no longer remember the hollow, deathly loneliness. The light inside her vibrated around her. When she spoke, they were her First Words. "Thank You," she said, hearing her self for the first time. "Thank You." She saw her face in the mirror for the first time. Her eyes sparkled blue, like their origins, like the sea, like the sky. Her face shaped like her mother's, her skin like cream. She could say hello now to her mother, and for the first time in ten years, she could hear her mother say hello back. She shivered, again and again at the divinity of it all. Then she called one person, she called her mother's last remaining sister and she said, "Nothing is ever going to be the same again," and without hesitation her mother's sister said "I know." Then she said, "Thank God. I was so worried."

"You don't have to be anymore," said the girl, and then she almost hung up before the Aunt said, "Hey, I am going to take this ride with you."

"Although," she laughed, "I have no earthly idea where we are going." They both knew that it was right, and the crevasse between them, once filled with the death and the drugs, closed over. The girl said, "I think we're going back where we all came from, and I think that place is really, really good."

[Turning in and facing your own pain/

Is turning in and facing the Planet's Pain

You must heal yourself to Heal the Earth.]

Later Winter, 2012. Free Union, Virginia

Pele.

So I've told you what happened to me the first morning in Hawaii, how I slept walked into Black Death beach with the stones of my past in my pockets like Virginia Woolf on her last swim, and I was caught in that rip and saved by a Tibetan monk and a Kundalini teacher who told me Pele had taken my breath as an offering. I learned that the Goddess Pele lives inside of every woman, she's our fire and she's who we've been taught to fear and stifle because her energy is both creative and destructive. We fear our own fire, we fear that chaotic power that lives inside of us. Life itself is the cycle of creation and destruction, so we fear life. Like kundalini, Pele sleeps inside us, and when she wakes you can either do your best to deny it or you can accept her thrilling, mystifying, chakra-blasting offer to awaken to your possibility. To deny her is to deny the goddess inside you and to continue to suffer. "If you bring forth what is within you, what you bring forth will save you. If you do not bring forth what is within you, what you do not bring forth will destroy you." The Gospel of Thomas.

So that first morning I walked with a pull toward the water, I even got a ride from an old lady dressed in white, who they say, mythically, is an embodiment of Pele herself. And that morning, for some reason, I had dressed in all black. I haven't done that really since I woke up, I've been so attracted to rich colors and fabric, but I felt somber as I dressed and reached for dark. I know scared a lot of you with that story, but now comes the beautiful bookend of the trip. On my last night in Hawaii I was lounging by the pool with three friends, we were all at peace and processing the great soul work we'd done, we lounged topless in seventy five degree weather with a breeze rustling through the palm trees, we would rise from the cool pool to steam in the hot tub, and we gathered in the grass to talk about our journeys. One of the girls had the idea to go to the closest town to buy wine and find a place to watch the sunset.

The group was headed to the car, but I ran back to my room- it felt important, suddenly, to dress for the occasion. I dressed in all white, something I've also rarely done. I fished out these soft white pure silk pants that I had bought last minute before the trip, and had yet to wear. A few days before I left they plummeted from $180 to $19 (my lucky blessed number) on Anthropologie and I snagged them. I put on a white tank and threw on a long white sweater. We piled in the car, and we drove toward the only store near by, a tiny part of the island that had not been destroyed by the last volcano, this tiny sacred patch of land that been spared and therefore become that much holier to the people of Puna. Across from the little market there was a path to the newest beach on the Island, Pele had carved it out with her last eruption. They say if you walk all the way out to that point that it's the cleanest air in the entire world. Dusk was beginning to settle and we had no flashlights, so the other girls waited on the path, they didn't want to get all the way down to the water and then not be able to find their way back in the dark. But I had this feeling I was beginning to find my way through the dark.

Again I felt the pull, this one big and undeniable. "I'll be right back," I said, and took off. I was walking barefoot on Pele's black crunchy lava rocks and the air was so cool and fresh and sweet and everything was the color of violet, the color of the Divine. I walked further and deeper along the path, not sure how much longer I would have to go before I saw the opening to this brand new beach, but when I got there I gasped. Empty and waiting, it looked like the end of the earth, like the first and last beach in the world, and I stood there while the wind picked up my hair and her tingling touch danced across my skin, and out over the expanse of the silky black water the moon's magical milky light leaked across the sea. As far as I could see on the sides of me there were only these towering dramatic black cliffs, everything bathed in the hazy violet velvety air and illuminated by the moon. The wind picked up harder, and I sucked in air that was sweeter than I had ever tasted, and I rose my arms to the sea and said "thank you," and then there was a voice.

"YOU ARE HERE. YOU MADE IT."

It was the voice of my ancestors, it was the voice of Pele, it was the voice of God, of mother earth, of mother moon, of mother ocean , of nature, of life. It was my own. The one I have been seeking, that has been calling to me all these years. I felt more love-big big all consuming powerful love— than I ever had in my 33 years, and more breath, surging life-force, in my body than I ever experienced. I knew I was ancient, and I knew I was part of this ancient magic, and I knew I belonged, that I was needed and essential. I knew I had been missed, loved, longed for, and I was being received. In my honoring I was being honored, awash in the violet light of the divine. One must be divine to converse with the divine.

That breath I had lost on the first morning in the water was returned, it was returned with the force of a thousand angels, goddesses, witches, mystics, shamans and their magic light and force surged through me, each cell was so awake it was dancing pulsating exploding with light. When the darkness finally fell, I was fully awake. And it fell in perfect time, as if the angels had held up the canopy of the night sky for this meeting, and I fell to my knees in thanks in lust and in love for this life, and I turned back around transformed, with new cells, with new love, and as I was walking back every single chakra surged open, and my seventh, like my first kundalini awakening, was shattered open the widest, as if I had a true halo of white light. Holly and Natalie were waiting on the path, standing there, smiling at me. I didn't need light to see, the moon and my own body were bright enough.

"How was it?" they asked.

At first I didn't have any words, and then the kundalini ran up and down my spine and I said, shaking, "it was the most beautiful thing I have ever seen in my life," and then I just started to convulse in tears of joy and peace, and the three of us stood there, holding each other, shaking and crying with joy. "We knew something was happening, we could feel it," they said. "I love your big beautiful brave heart," Natalie said.

I wore black that first morning, for the funeral of my old life, when Pele drowned my dead self and the past, and I wore white for the rising, the meeting and the merging, white for my initiation into my true self and the Divine.

[She said, "If you want to learn how to live/ study the dying/ everyone else is lying."]

Spring, 2012, Free Union, Virginia

Roadside Burial.

Last night I had dinner with my little blond cousin and her friends, we sat outside at a Mexican restaurant in breezeless sweater weather, we shared a gigantic plate of nachos and talked about individual awakenings and the universal waking. And we talked about the part of the journey, my reiki master calls the Spiritual Trenches. This is where the hardest work is done. This is the part where you're terrified of changing your whole life and your new path seems like an experiment that could go deadly wrong, and you're wondering if you've made it all up. But the old ways stop working at all. When you rely on old coping or defense mechanisms, and do things that work against your personal alignment, Love's alignment, or ignore your instinct, you get burned, badly. ["I told you so," said your Instinct.]

You keep telling yourself, "I've come too far to go back now. I've come too far to go back now," but there are parts of you that still shake with uncertainty on the bridge from the old life the new, that one you have to walk all alone.

On my drive home around eleven I swerved to miss an animal lying in the road, I gasped in sadness when I saw it was the little black and white cat. I had seen this cat roaming the neighborhood and trying to cross this road before. I don't know if she belonged to a person or just to nature. I swung the car back around and drove back, I wanted to make sure she wasn't still alive, and if she was dead, to at least get her off the road so no one would hit her again. When I touched her, she was stiff, her mouth open, blood running out. There was no energy in the body. All the parts were there, but no Divine force. Last Fall in the Berkshires I was hiking Monument Mountain and I saw a dead mouse on the path. Perhaps it died right then, for I saw the spirit move from the mouse up into the air. From the middle of the road I picked the cat up and laid her in a ditch on the side of the road, and I held my hands over her and asked the Great Spirits to ensure her peace and safety in her soul's journey. I could feel her around me in the air. When I got home the dogs rushed to the door, smelling death on my hands.

Since the full moon I've been tossing all night in bed, and last night I woke up a few times with her face, frozen, in my mind, the picture of death. But this morning in the backyard, like Whitman says, the powerful play goes on, and you will contribute a verse.

It is most certainly Spring, the world is more awake and alive than it has been in half a year, it is warm, almost hot, and the birds are here in droves, blue jays and robins chirping and flirting and flapping, butterflies vibrating around each other and buds that were long-held, incubating in the dark womb of the earth are appearing in orgasmic colors in the grass and on the trees. The black and white kitty will decompose back into this earth from which she nurtured herself and stalked with her soft padded feet, and eventually all of us will follow her back into Mother Earth. The roots her veins, the dirt her flesh, the trees her lungs. I am sorry this kitty died during springtime. Every death is a reminder of life, I am grateful for her reminder. I wish I could say something more beautiful for the cat, but the only thing I know to say is the aren't we so lucky to be here. Here is the one thing my friend Kianna and I have been hearing when we seek our answers: "Self-love is the path. Forgive yourselves." Please forgive yourself. Please. Awaken along with Mother Earth this Spring, Allow yourself the fullest life possible.

I like watching children play, it reminds me how to live. I love how when the rain starts to fall, they don't run inside and hide. Instead they laugh and play in it and they don't fear getting wet. I like when they fall down , unashamedly, let themselves feel it, they don't hide the pain. Then a moment later they get up, move on, and it's been released and forgotten. I like how when they meet someone or something new or different, they look them in the eyes, and not down with judgement, instead they are lit up by delight and curiosity. When did they start to hold on to the pain and the fear, like a security blanket from life? When will I shed mine? What good has it done me?

Addendum. I watch the surfers to remember that the rise and fall is all part of the dance of life. I watch them to remember how to rise after the fall so fearlessly like children who fall from horses softly with trust and don't break a bone. And then the heart stays open and they don't fear life, they don't fear experience, they don't fear the ride. And so they ride on. The human spirit is tremendously buoyant. Adults fall contracted in fear and shatter and they never get back on again. And the heart closes and they fear life, they fear experience, they are terrified of getting hurt, of loss rejection, failure. So they stop. They get stuck in the story of the hurt. They stop living and they stop loving and they stop reaching and they stop playing. They lose their courage and sense of curiosity and adventure, which life is supposed to be. Have you seen how a child will fall, cry for two seconds, then two seconds later she smiles and says "let's do it again." Children are my teachers. And these surfers. The endless rise and fall and the grace and trust of it all. Trust is so graceful. Faith is so serene. The human spirit is tremendously buoyant. I watch them follow a wave like intuition, letting some pass and saying yes to others. And some carry them all the way to shore. But the shore isn't the destination, the wave is. The ride is. The sea itself, life itself, is. Don't fear the fall.

***

[There's something so wildly untamable about you {And I Love it.) You're a force of nature. And forces of nature cannot be stopped. You help me remember my lost wild. They wild they took from us. When we stopped believing in our own power an or own magic. So please whatever you do: Don't forget you're magic/ And Stay wild Child.]

Spring, 2012, Free Union, Virginia

Working on My Roots

I haven't given a damn about my hair for a long time, I've been so focused on cleaning up the internal, but this moon's light being so close to full is making me see myself clearly, too clearly, and I felt messy, too messy. So today I started from the outside, and I went to the hair salon downtown and as soon as I got there the stylist went into ER mode, if she could have laid me on a stretcher and hooked my hair up to an oxygen tank, she would have. For her I was in critical condition, this was a cut/color/gloss/layer emergency and I let her do her thing, as long as I could shut my eyes and not think. But I'm no good at that. So with her fingers in my roots I started thinking about my psychological, spiritual roots at home here in Virginia. I came home in November- well to the outskirts of home, to this farmhouse twenty minutes away- to re- root. At Kripalu my muladhara (root chakra) was crying out for some stability and home made sense. I see now why I was called home, and I am grateful for these last four or five months. I have done what I set out to accomplish, to be by my best friend's side during her happy time of engagement, to get to know my father again as an adult, to picnic in the places of my defeats as I heard someone say. My best friend and I do lovely dinners. My father and I do these great country runs. I sat at my mother's grave on the cold lonely hillside in January.

But this is not my life anymore, there is no life here for me anymore. The more I think about roots, the more I think about how deeply complicated they are. They are knotted, and gnarly, rock hard and endlessly deep, twisted and intertwined forever with the roots of others. Mine are deeply, deeply twisted. Last night I felt I almost drowned in my past, it is so rich and deep here, and at times it is so incredibly dark. I was a child as these events unfolded, I had no concept of choice, but I do now. But sometimes it feels like so long ago and another life, sometimes it doesn't feel like anytime's gone by at all.

Facing your biggest fears is the key to life. I think we have to look at fear and pain differently, as messengers. I search hard for the right composition of strength and vulnerability. I am too vulnerable in some areas, too defended and built up in others. The March Full Moon is low and almost full, she'll be all the way lit come Thursday. They say this "Storm Moon" makes us a little crazier than usual, it stirs us up inside, and I feel it. I look so polished and smooth on the outside today, but inside the darkness is surfacing,and fighting it is fruitless. The moon is our greatest mirror, when she is full, in turn she reveals us in full. Not just the pretty stuff, the edited stuff, or your best side. The warts. The unhealed wounds. No photoshop. Last night in yoga class I was asked to invite every one inside me to the party— not just my strengths, like my my bliss, my laughter, my love and compassion, these things I proudly display. No the invite list was much longer— she asked we also invite everything inside we try to hide, stifle, fight or avoid. For me, that means inviting my gluttony, my ego, my impatience, my darkness, and my reactiveness. Oh, and who are we kidding, my mother issues and my own fear of abandonment. I barely had to look around for them, this moon has them in the spotlight. Begrudgingly, embarrassed and ashamed of them, I invited them to the party. This is natural to fear/shun/hate these things inside of us. This is how we are bred, and this is what we have to unlearn. Everyday we are each different and every day the mission for these letters is different, but I largely write on a mission of self-acceptance and self love— that means not just the pretty days. My teacher Shakti Sunfire would call this "radical self-acceptance." I think it's pretty radical to love yourself at your lowest, I think it's pretty radical to still call yourself a warrior when you've been beat.

It's acceptance. And then comes relief. Its surrender. You don't realize how exhausted you are from the internal war. It's about letting it all in the door. The more I tell my ugly truths NO, don't come in, stay out in the cold dark, the harder they will bang at the door, and eventually, they will get in with a force much greater than had I let them in, and it will blow my house down, taking innocent others with it. So instead I invite them in now, when I can. Come in, darkness, dance with my light. Come in pain of my mother, come in pain of my broken heart. My joy and my sorrow are bedmates. Had I not gone through hell, I wouldn't know heaven. My roots show the knots and scars, the pain of my past. I see them. I acknowledge them. I try my best, to accept them, eventually I hope to love them. I refuse to be afraid of who I am or what's happened to me or what I have done anymore. The more I understand these things, the less they frighten me. My roots, my choices, and my sources of pain, are like any child, any person, any animal, the more I accept them, the less they cry out.

I don't want to delude myself that this is still some sort of rehearsal. I know that life is happening now, and it is my choice to rise to the occasion or not. I am ready, awake, and up to this challenge to love myself in full. I hope you join me. I applaud you and your courage, whether you're at the top of the mountain or entering the dark cave, it doesn't matter. Whether the wound is fresh or healing, I applaud you. Keep going. I applaud you and your work. I applaud you and your journey. I applaud you and your pain. Keep moving through the fire.

[I try to explain being Sourced, becoming a Source-eress, as, “we're just like a lamp or a DVD player," I say. Whenever we say of our lives, "I can't get it to work," like we do with a piece of electronic equipment. And the answer is usually, "well did you plug it in?" For me, we're each like lightning rods for the Divine. But we have to plug in to work well. But we have to get still, get quiet, and plug in, for our positive light energy to flow out, for us to Shine. Find your ritual your quiet moment inside, and access the Divine. Plug into the Universe to light up the world.]

Spring, 2012. Free Union, Virginia

Dirty Laundry.

Because people whom I love and respect greatly are bravely airing out their dirty laundry, and because one person's liberation leads to another's, I'm gonna empty one of these dark black bags I've been carrying around. It's spring cleaning time for the body and soul and I am definitely aware it's time to clean out my heart and lighten my load as I am headed back to the Island. For me, that means telling a story, something I've been keeping out of fear and shame. For the last two weeks I have been locked in the great battle for courage and all of this pain-facing is part of it. Helmet on, Armor locked, Sword/Pen in Hand, Here Goes the story of my last Dark Night.

When I got to the Island, I was a mess. I had absolutely no idea who I was, and I hated the person I was pretending to be. Had I had any idea who I REALLY was, I would have rushed to meet her. It was my last option, I had no where else to go after 30 years of pain and destruction. I came there to heal, but healing doesn't happen just by stepping foot on sacred healing soil. First, all the shit has to surface. And then you gotta face it. And own it. And you gotta make some big decisions, and do some major house cleaning. Responsibility. How I ended up taking a chance to live there is Divine in itself, before I had any sense of the Divine.

Thanks to my father's mother, our family has had this magical cabin on a cool and leafy dirt road that drops you off right at the beach, it was my mother's favorite place. It is mystical, it is magical, it is healing.

My hard-working father loves it. He can only get up there for 2 weeks a summer but those are the finest days of his year, in the sun, in the canoe, on the bike, on the grill, on the porch, on the sand that cuts between the warm still pond and the magnificent refreshing and tremendous ocean. My mother and father, two very different people, both loved it like a fairytale land. My love for the Island was maybe the one thing I inherited from them both.

I moved there when my "real" life had kicked my heart and my ass- after the losses of my mother and aunt, my fiancé had left me in October 2009. I spent the darkest winter of my life in a slummy apartment in Brooklyn, when the situation got out of control with a raging, misogynistic, racist, schizophrenic landlord, I moved out in fear of him, breaking my lease, and he threatened to kill me. In fear, how I was mostly motivated almost all the time, the agenda to simply survive, I fled. My passion for life, my career, and love was dead. I was alone at the bottom of my life, in a dark well,, shaking and drinking the whole way, still desperately in love with my ex. Loving someone like that when they don't love you? Close as it gets to a coffin. My worst fear, being buried alive. And it happened. One day I was on the back porch of Gramma's house, lying in the sun, trying to still my thoughts enough to read a paperback, drinking a glass of white wine, God forbid I waited until dinner, when the Tom Petty song "Wildflowers" came on the local radio station. I had heard the song a million times before, but this song came in so loud and clear, it was like the Universe muted absolutely everything else, all my thoughts, any other distractions. I see now it was a PAY ATTENTION moment.

You belong among the wildflowers/You belong in a boat out at sea

Sail away, kill off the hours/You belong somewhere you feel free

Run away, go find a lover/Run away, let your heart be your guide

You deserve the deepest of cover/You belong in that home by and by

You belong among the wildflowers/You belong somewhere close to me

Far away from your trouble and worry/You belong somewhere you feel free

I ached at the mere idea of your heart being your guide. I had no idea JUST how much fear ruled my life. I ached at the word "belong." Belonging… I longed to belong. I belonged no where, to no one, to nothing.

Now I know what was calling me, who I am and where I belong as a participant in the Universe—not some geographic place but the Soul's Home, Me, my ancient self was sending out messages whenever it could catch my scattered attention. Don't Give Up. You Belong. We are Crying Out for You. Please Come Home.

Because of that song, I called my father.

"Dad, I want to stay here." His response, and a lot of responses, were, that is where you go to vacation, not where you live. [P.S. "Rules" like that aren't real. Do what your heart says.] He was worried. Everyone was worried. But I had to make a big, drastic change. Radical change takes radical courage. There was no going back. There was nothing to go back to. So I stayed, and it was absolutely a year of magical healing.

But first—I was a mess. I was still getting really drunk, I even slept with someone dangerous when I was blacked out— and it was really scary. I'd say it was rock bottom. It was far from the first time but it was the last time. The final end. End of the binge drinking, end of the pill popping and the first punch through the darkness, because I woke up days before my 31st birthday and my bare knees hit the dusty wooden floor and I asked for Help. AND I GOT IT.

This was my first meeting with what I now know as Goddess. That is when the magic started to happening. Soon after I met someone and I fell for him, and months later- just at the point I had begun to trust him and us— he broke up with me in a three line email. I was not ready for that, spiritually not fit enough for the test. I was taking it well, until I told a few friends, and listened to them instead of me. "GET MAD," they said. "Be offended." "Demand an answer." That's the really dangerous thing. When you're newly forming, and the world screams come back to your old role. Be like the rest of us and re-act in all your old patterns. And that was the beginning of the emotional rabbit hole I went down, My Ego was reawakened, and my old victim patterns too. I was still very much grieving my fiancé and all the love-loss ripped the wound open and rolled into one powerfully destructive storm. Still so new to my path — I let my Ego take over. I lost the power of choice. Things were darkening again. A few weeks later, still stewing in what felt like a betrayal— an old friend came to the island- and I decided to go out with her. I felt betrayed by my spiritual path as well, like, "what had it done for me," I had done all this work and it felt like it was only leading me into alienation. So I tantrumed, I wanted to feel "normal" and go back to my partying ways. I wanted to connect with her, I was going through so many big

Kundalini changes and not my "old self" and I didn't know how to talk about regular things, so I tried through alcohol.

So after over six months of a living a loving and healthy life, I drank two bottles of wine on an empty stomach in the hot sun. That night, wasted, I tried to explain my Kundalini awakenings for the first time to my very rational practical friend who only knew the old me. Very dangerous. Nothing could have been more wrong about the time, place, or circumstances. I had NO idea what was happening to me I just knew I - and the entire way I saw the world- was rapidly changing. Wasted, I was going on about the Light. Angels. God. She freaked out, I got very upset, scared, and defensive. After she went home, I was so angry and alone- so, I did the worst thing I could do. Late that night, I headed to my ex's house wanting a real answer- and walked right into an emotional beat down. It was so painful. He wouldn't even answer the door, he called from the stairs and told me to go. I'm pretty sure he called me crazy. And I was so so terrified of being crazy. I definitely was no longer normal. I don't think I had ever been but I just couldn't hide it anymore.

Waking up alone with a broken ego and spirit, the next morning was one of the hardest yet. I had been rejected by an old friend and a lover in one night, and it had all been my fault, because of my actions. The blow was massive. I didn't just fall off my path, it was like a drunkenly moshpitted into darkness. And absolutely everyone moved away as I fell, so I hit the cold cement, hard. I felt shoved into a steel dungeon with the door slammed shut after me. These were the trenches. I was deeply, painfully, ashamed of myself. I thought of death again, death at my own hands. I allowed the one night to overshadow my many months of spiritual growth. I tried to continue to love my life on the Island but everything around me started to fall apart after that, my living situation exploded (already a fragile situation at best) and I realized I was in no place to heal others. I was too skinny and wild and completely ungrounded from the Kundalini, it was time for me to seek a teacher but I had no idea— about how one goes about that, about any of this new spiritual life. I could feel myself standing on the cliff, it was time to fly, but I dragged my feet, not wanting to leave the Island out of fear. I just didn't want to run anymore- even though I knew it was time to go. When you refuse to make a choice, one will be made for you. I received a final swift kick to the back when I ran into my ex at an open market. The way he looked at and spoke to me, like I was nothing, like a mistake. For a moment, I wanted to sink right through the ground. But then something else happened.

I felt Goddess around me. She's who found me on the floor last December, and she's also what wrapped around me in the market air in early summer. I know her feeling now, I see her when I need her, when I meditate, but sometimes she takes the reigns and calls to me. In meditations she's appeared as a divine, holy beautiful woman in white with her feet inches off the ground. Serene, smiling, powerfully beautiful and blissful, she is my highest self.

But after that I fled the Island for Kripalu, which was most certainly the right thing to do. Things started to make sense again— I made sense. People spoke my language. I didn't look back until I was in Hawaii, a half a year later, when it was clear my path was leading me back to the Island. When I allowed myself to miss it, I realized the land and sprit has been calling me back, I've loved it and known it my whole life, my first summer ever was spent there in my mother's womb, 33 years ago. The island's waters have healed me again and again and I look forward to cleaning my soul in them all summer. I am in the major healing stages still, I have great work to do. But I continue to walk through the fear and the darkness, and toward the light and toward my heart's calling. As far as I am concerned, this is the only direction to walk.

"Don't move the way fear makes you move.

Move the way love makes you move.

Move the way joy makes you move." Osho

When you allow yourself to grieve you allow the natural process all life needs- by allowing winter, you allow spring. You've got to go in to get out. If you don't go to the funeral inside yourself-if you put off facing the pain of the loss for years—then you're stuck and holding up the natural cycles of your life. Life around you goes on, while you stay somewhere back where you got hurt or things got real dark. Last night I mourned and buried something I have been running from for years. That load is lighter today. The path appears much broader. The letting go was and is real.

I talked to my astrologer on the phone the other day and she told me something to the extent of this: "It's time to stop waiting by the door, it's time to leave the house despite the fear of storms. You have made it through the worst of the storms. You can go outside and live now."

I understand holding on too long to pain. In the past I have even let my pain define me. But if we can throw the loss a funeral, where we pull up a seat or a pew and honor the loss, look at it and say goodbye, even allow the feeling of "failing" or fear because that person or old dream is no longer in your life, we can begin to start to heal. And then healing, I've learned, can happen much faster than we think.

So when the pain of this loss comes knocking again, it's nothing more than a reminder it's waiting to be let go. Don't run from the knock, don't run from the fear of the pain. Sit with it. It's seeking your attention for a reason, it wants to leave your emotional body. It's seeking its send-off. If you get the courage to have a funeral for this old dream, if you hold for yourself a final ritual in which you allow yourself to say goodbye, then afterwards you can head in your black dress and your pearls to the brunch in someone's large living room seeped in light, and everyone can get a little tipsy on mimosas and bring up only the best of times, and maybe some people will even laugh, laugh so hard they cry and then keep doing both, because both feels most fitting. [She held a funeral for her unworthiness, the reception was a smashing success]. Then the next day you don't wake up and go to the funeral again, because you've paid your respects and you've honored the loss. No, the next day, you start really living your life again, honoring life again. This is ceremony, ritual. It marks and honors the passage of time. Of your very life. This stuff is important.

My friend walked a bridge in the night in the midwest and let go of her lost love, dropped his name into the river. He eventually came back to her, but in the time in between she was able to let go and fully live her life. Who knows if living her life to the fullest brought him back- this is not about the other person, this is about ourselves.

Whatever happened, performing the ritual meant letting go to make room for something better. We can all hold these ceremonies for ourselves and our "dead". You can let go in many, many ways. Part with the dead inside you so you can move on without the dead weight- and the dead wait. The more you make confront and make peace with and part with the dead parts of yourself- old dreams, old hurts, old assumptions, old ways- inside you, the more awake and alive you really are in the present. It's a soul bath. Remember, again, there is no right way to do ritual, it's all about intention.

So last night, instead of doing what I always do, which is say "I should really let that go," "I've got to let that go," but never really doing it, I stopped and held space and time to see it go. This wasn't not painful. There was stuff I had not wanted to see- but it was no where near as bad as I had imagined all these years. But I stayed in the fire until it cooled. With a candle lit, a rose quartz on my chest and a reiki hand on my solar plexus, I held ceremony. It was waiting to say goodbye, it asked for my attention and I finally gave it to it. This thing had been waiting in the door way for years for me to let it go. I finally let it out, like a trapped bird who had been banging around inside me, desperate for a way out, dying to fly. Like a woman on her deathbed, asking for peace. Forgiving all and everyone, especially herself.

[If you learned/ You didn't lose.]

Spring, 2012, Free Union, Virginia

Leaving the South Once More.

I am getting ready to leave the south for that magic New England island again, and I am walking around with the feelings of tying things up and saying goodbye. I am looking deeper at my father's face and drinking in the grace and strength of my girlfriends. I am memorizing the winding roads lined by the divine Blue Ridge mountains and savoring the sounds I hear out in the country quiet. I love the moans of the cows in the pastures and the cries of the Canadian Geese as they fly over this open land. The calls of these geese are my favorite sounds in nature. Something in me returns home every time I hear them. Stir that with the rustling wind and the wind chimes twinkling and I'm one happy earth goddess. Last night I heard those geese and I rushed to the window to look for them- but every time, for the last four months, I have missed them by a moment, and they fly over the house like phantoms I can only hear and never see. This morning, very early, I had Lisa's favorite Mary Oliver poem "Why I Wake Early" in my head, and I was moved to walk. I greeted the day wrapped in her soft cream sweater and electric pink leggings and walked down the road as the sun was still taking her seat in the sky, stretching her long and wispy pink and yellow fingers across its endless expanse. Lisa used to walk to the beach with her dog every morning. When you're up that early it feels like you're having a secret, silky and intimate affair the world while everyone else still sleeps. You're part of sacred shamanic cult. You can whisper secrets and she'll whisper them back. Mary Oliver says to the dawn, "Hello you who made the morning, watch, now, how I start the day in happiness, in kindness." This morning in Virginia the air felt like Lisa's Rhode Island beach, soft and summery, and as Gracie and I rounded the bend we stopped at an empty cow pasture, which was absolutely filled with Canadian Geese. A field full of them, as if they ruled the land. I didn't finally get to see one goose, I got to see one hundred. Gracie laid down in the grass as I stood on the old wooden fence and watched them.

Again, I said "Thank you."

Wrapped in Lisa's sweater like a hug, I do not have to look hard to find her. My late aunt was the woman who showed me, by example, that anyone can change her life. Had I not seen her do it, I am not sure I could have. I read some of my old journals this morning while I had coffee on my bed. I see that I used to "live" like I was in a coffin, everything was black and there was no freedom and no possibility and no future. Certainly, no present. Alive, but not living. Boxed up and good as dead. It was like my reiki healer once said to me when I lived in Santa Monica, "You live by the ocean, yet you never let yourself go in." Sometimes when I am taking this life for granted I close my eyes and pretend I'm buried again and forever. That this life is over and I am confined to a dark wooden box underground. I hold this thought till it hurts, then I open my eyes, and I can't believe where I am. I can't believe the trees, I can't believe the sky. I can't believe the touch of Gracie's fur. Truly, this is a magical kingdom. Awake, alive, and glittering. If you are buried, I pray for you to be brave, to rise from your grave. I pray that you will forgive yourself and that you will free yourself and that you will let yourself live. I pray that you will allow yourself the ocean and the stars, let life, let you, be as wide as deep as the sea as wide and deep as the galaxy. Just take one chance, just take one step, and see where it leads you. Today is the full moon, and if we all were - and we are—ancient shamans and goddesses and good witches we would gather around our great bonfire and toss in all our love and dreams and all the pain too, from the past. Offer it all up to the Gods, and we would dance, and sing, and hold hands, and hold each other. Tonight in my heart I'll hold a bonfire under the Full Moon for each of you. Let's toss it all in. Let's watch it all burn, let's offer it something Higher. Let's dance and love like we're on fire.

[Threshold.

Don't you see/

It's all been leading Up to this/

The fire has burned away

/ All your old skins.

You stand in the new skin

/ Naked at the door way

/ The Threshold.

Where you take a breath/

and release the old.

Choose the mystery of life, and/

You carry yourself over/

This is where/

The Fire-walking Truly Starts/

You're on the bridge baby/

So don't look back/

And stop looking down/

Because it's only / Up/ From here.]

Spring, Free Union, Virginia, 2012.

Dear You, It's Me.

Dear Lost and Lonely Girl running in McCarren Park in the dead of February,

The snow is dirty and stale and the air feels like ice, stinging and slapping your face, and somehow you feel you deserve it. You expect pain, so you get it. You're blocks from your dingy basement apartment, the first place you've ever lived alone, at 30 years old. And it's awful, I know, with its drunken raging landlord and its dirty leaky everything. Maybe this is all temporary, you think, maybe he's coming back. And you went back to New York because that's where you once had a big booming life before your fiancé, that's where he fell in love with you and you thought maybe you could be that girl again— but you have learned the ugly truth about never going home again. You're a ghost in a city where you once felt lit up and center stage. It's so terrible it's added to all your doubts that you should even be allowed to make decisions for yourself, and now, completely alone and abandoned, you're sure you won't ever be safe. And now you're out running, the cold air searing your tiny ragged lungs, the dog is slipping on the ice, and everything is a battle, when one of his songs comes on your iPod. Him screaming about how you don't know how to love. How you ask for things you can't give. You became the whipping girl of his songs, but you haven't even erased all of his music yet because you refuse to imagine or live a life without him, you don't know how, this is your last piece of him. So you start crying while you're running, in the cold and unforgiving air and you fall down, your legs just give out. You're too weak. And since you can't be any lower, you decide to text him. Even on runs, you keep your phone on you at all times, just in case he calls you, or emails you, or texts you, which he never, ever does. But you reach out to him after trying not to for a week or so. You say you miss him so much you can't breathe. In a moment he texts back and for that moment there is hope in the corpse of your heart: but all he writes is: "Being alone is hard on everyone." You will never forget the clinical tone of that text. You say nothing, there is nothing to say. It falls on you like a beam of steel, you're trapped under the mean cold weight of it, the hard-hitting lack of love for you that you still refuse to believe, even when he writes to you like a stranger he hates, because that love once burned so bright. That love that once felt big as the sky, is now a hole in your heart, as big as the sky. Finally you get up and you crawl back to that rat's nest, and you lie down, and you hope you never wake up again.

So… Hey You!! I've been meaning to write you for some time, but honestly, I've just been so busy I couldn't find the time. My moments are so precious to me, I swallow my life up greedily, with an unquenchable thirst. Whoops I sound like one of those bubbly happy people you hate because you're so jealous of. I'm sorry [but not really, mostly that you feel jealousy, because it only ever hurts you, why don't you use it instead as inspiration, that it's showing you something you desire?] But there's another reason I haven't reached out: you live in the past, and I don't play with the past, I work hard not to pick at those wounds. You wish the past was a portal you could step into and return to that old life. You are banging at the walls with bloody fists, looking for that secret trap door back. You can keep trying to live in the past, but I'm pretty sure that's a slow descent to death.

I have to write fast, because there's so much to do, there's so much I wanna do. I know that sounds so foreign: we used to hate the hours as they ticked by, the wretched lonely hours without him, filling them was torture. Now, I authentically tell you, sweet girl, that I love the hours, filled with magical moments and incessant possibility— I have learned of miracles that are available to each and every person, for instance, if you stay present, absolutely anything is possible. That probably sounds like it's written in German.

You're probably watching Law and Order SVU re-runs, laid up on the couch, where you also sleep, because the bed is too lonely. You're dying to feel nothing, listening to the landlord scream next door, you're finished with one bottle of red and eyeing your second. Why not, you think. You've got nothing, there's nothing to lose. I haven't had a TV in so long because it bores me, life is much more interesting. Watching TV is numbing, and I want to be a constant participant and witness. TV's also a portal to a very sick society that I want no part in, in fact my passion is to heal that society. You are a prime victim of that society. Pills, possessions, pain, hate, fear...

So yes, my days are a little different than yours, I'm reading or writing or running or doing yoga or talking to other women about the power of self love and transformation, women I don't "know" but I do, because here's the thing, we're all one. We're all on the same journey. And I'm still you, you're a part of me, but I hold you in my arms like a battlefield orphan. I am holding you in my arms and I am running you over the border that falls between the dark and the light.

I want to tell you, this past you're dying and mourning for, that you're scraping and screaming at the walls of time because you want it back so bad— this grief that's making your hair fall out and making you drink so much you go blind at night, it was the best thing ever happened to you. Don't hate me, I know how you hate words like this that seem to try to tie your pain up neatly. You think no one can understand your pain. But it's me. I lived it with you, if you can call that living. And I still say it was the best thing that ever happened to you. I wish you hadn't been so completely Bell Jar about it, I wish you could have gone through this passage with a tiny bit of grace, but there again is a lesson, about letting go gracefully so your arms can welcome the new, brighter, bigger things. Everything has its time. Everything has its season. Everything has its reason.

I understand now that sometimes in this life we have to die to be reborn again. Sometimes it's tiny daily deaths and rebirths like the rise and fall of waves, or sometimes, like you, right now, it's the Big One. The Tsunami, the Big Huge Shipwreck break down. He was the iceberg that ripped you open. So this isn't news to you, because you're scared senseless and for good reason: your ship is headed for the final disaster. He knew that ship was sinking, he got himself to safety. It doesn't matter, we all have to be born and die alone. We have to die with what we've done and who we've been and how we've loved. You're always with you, haven't you noticed? There is no escaping you. If you hate yourself and feel you've done nothing with your life except ruin it, this is most certainly the scariest part.

Let me tell you about the shore you wake up on, after you've drowned. Let me tell you about this bright- and at this time- very distant shore, where you will awaken, where you actually find out what it means to be alive. Let me tell you about the girl who rises out of the water. In the two years since he came home from tour and told you in the dead of night in that Santa Monica apartment that he said he simply didn't love you anymore and to not cry because you were embarrassing yourself- you've been in love again. [It was brief and messy but full of great sex and great lessons]. You've lived by the ocean on an animal rescue farm, where you all rescued each other on a daily basis, and you've been to a spiritual healing place called Kripalu- you went so much because it felt like home. You found others like you. No more wearing masks or costumes, you spoke the same language of light. There, you attained your reiki master. Reiki was the only thing that ever healed you in your old life, and now you embody it. You found out yoga wasn't just for rich skinny tan girls— no yoga was for you. Sweet yoga. And you've been to Hawaii, you flew by yourself for ten days and it only whet your appetite for more travel, more adventure, and to see this great big beautiful world that you once felt so cut off from. Your self love [what's that, you ask] became Universal love. That's the power of love. It's so big. It's what the Universe runs on. It never runs out. You have yet to really taste its power. It's gonna blow you away the way no backstage bender ever could. Now you're signed up to go back to the ocean and become a yoga teacher. When you stopped writing about famous people for a living you started writing about yourself, and you found yourself. You're really, really lovely. You're full of grace and power. You feel the power of the ocean and the mountains inside of you. You see this in everyone and everything. You have a Universe inside of you, and it's mind-shatteringly eternal and infinite and beautiful.

Had you just given yourself a chance... But you never did. Perhaps you never had a choice. I don't blame you anymore. So the Universe stepped in- like REALLY in. Flooded in and took the wheel. You'll see, soon, that you are connected to everything. You'll see a path, a golden path. You'll see you were never ever alone. At this point in your life people have told you a lot of lies and backed out of a lot of promises, and that's because you have done all that too, you don't know yet that you get what you give. That it's all a reflection and you attract what you are.

You are still waiting like a beggar at the gates of life, because you feel you are owed or deserve something for your pain. But there's one thing you were told that wasn't a lie. You were loved. Totally and unconditionally.

So here I come, here comes your Self, and I'm coming to get you on the couch in Brooklyn. You might not recognize me in my self-reliance and peace, but trust me, I am you. I don't wear make up and I haven't given a damn about my hair in ages. It's long and unruly and I don't care who thinks I'm hot, but I'm more beautiful than ever. People stare at me— they say that happens when a woman becomes truly aligned with Self- and it makes my friends laugh when we're out in public. I'll be dressed like a child in bright shining colors, and I'll have crystals around my neck, one for healing and one for love (we never stop healing and we never stop learning how to love). I'll have a new tattoo on my arm, the spiritual warrior rune, a great arrow ancient warriors painted on their shields before battle for protection and strength. I serve the light now. I'll have a big turquoise ring on my finger, I found it in Hawaii the day I almost drowned, but was saved. It reminds me how not alone, how safe I am, even on the brink of death. I'll be smiling at you, a big bright smile, and my eyes will be all lit up. Some people say my blue eyes turn violet and my pupils turn to hearts when I'm really awake. I'll be making light jokes, because there's something funny about everything, but you won't be smiling, because it's hard to smile on so much Xanax and wine and thoughts of death, but I will, I'll be smiling because I know this is the beginning. This is where we are going to start. The pain is the bridge. The wound is the light. The destruction is the creation. I'll pick you up and I'll take you to the place you fear the most and the safest place I know. I'll take you inside of me. It's safe in here, it's quiet and peaceful and you're going to see what I'm made of. I'm made of strength, love, light and resilience. I'm made of the Universe.

I'm coming for you, and we're not just going to make it, and we're not just going to be fine. Everything is going to be better than your small, locked and poisoned head could ever imagine. The tears of pain will be replaced with tears of love, joy, and release. The loved ones who have died will move inside of you, you will feel the strength of your ancestors, you will feel the strength of the infinite Universe.

Cry now though, let it out. I've got you, and I'm holding you in my strong and healing arms. For now, baptize yourself in your own tears of pain. And then rise with me, indomitable. It has happened. You are safe, you have crossed over, have saved yourself. You have been through hell, and now, I'd like to show you heaven.

Love,

You.

[The witch said, "Baby baby baby One way to stop living that same old story is to stop telling it."

And the Guru said, "my child my child my child let it go and it will let you go."

And she asked, :when do I stop dying for the things I've done."

And the answer came, "When you choose to be free you will be, each of us each of us each of us holds our own key."]

Free Union, Virginia, Spring 2012.

At First It's Hard to Unlearn.

It is so hard at first to unlearn the patterns of your old life and your terrible ways of treating yourself and not think all your old thoughts. It's hard to go against the grain, to push back, on an entire society and make choices for yourself that no one else can understand. That only you can see. But you reserve the right to change. You reserve the right to change your life.

Sometimes I ask myself, and wonder if others think, that I might have made this whole spiritual journey up as an escape from "real life." But then that begs the question, what is real, and what is normal? Is normal my old life of suffering and fear? Is normal the life that almost killed me, because I followed the rules and lived locked in a mind of fear and judgment? Have I had a psychotic break because I live by the laws of love and peace now? In my mind, I've gone sane. The old life was my fiction, this life is my truth.

Anyway, does it really matter? Who's to say who's making what up? If this spiritual journey is not real, how come, since I have been on it, I have been so awake, healthy, and happy? How come my life is now so peaceful, when the "normal" one I lived was one car crash after another? If that's normal, never knowing myself, and in turn making choices that hurt myself and everyone around me, then I'm very blissful and happy to be strange. And I've seen, as I heal, I naturally heal those around me. Without doing anything but me.

Why do we care how others live their lives? As long as they are happy? When it comes down to it, when life screeches into perspective— those times when someone faces losing their life, gets seriously ill or hurt, or passes away, do we ask, "I hope she lived a life based on mass society's rules about reality?" Do we say, "I hope everyone accepted her and she fit in?" Or do we say, "I hope she was happy?"Haven't you noticed, they either say, "She was happy," and find solace that she lived happily, or they say, "Well, she wasn't happy," and find solace that she has passed, because she wasn't happy here. That's the whole key, what people say when you have left. That happiness is all that matters. And when you do what you love, you are happy. And when you are happy you make others happy. (And when you are sad you make others sad). People who don't love themselves are very dangerous people. Trust me, I've been one.

When my mother was passing from this life to the next her last words to me were "Find the joy." In my last words to her, I promised her I would. I tattooed this on my back and sought for joy in vain and in desperate, dangerous ways outside of myself for 14 years. [Despite the good intentions, I see the sad sentence I was setting myself up for, that joy was always behind me, and I was always looking back for it instead of around me]. When I finally gave up on the rules that were killing me and took respite in myself alone, I found the universe, and then I found the joy.

You won't have to worry about me. You might not recognize or understand all my choices, but I am happy. And that's all I want you to be. I hear the music. I am dancing. I hope you find the version of life that makes the most sense to you and your heart.

[She said, "The Goddess woke up in me/

And she wont go back to sleep/

Before I only crawled safely along the shore /

Now I only swim where it is deep."]

Late Spring, Martha's Vineyard, 2012.

I Still Have Bad Days

Here's what I am also learning, in addition to the days of the endless blue skies and wind in my hair, the goose-bump synchronicity and the cell-fulfilling sensation of lightwork, or lovework, is that I still have these "bad" days. I still have these days like today, where everything the yoga teacher during training says feels like being scolded and feels personal. Where when trying to reach the bank about your stolen debit card (all your money) but you keep getting disconnected, so you continue to eat pasta with butter alone for the fifth day in a row, standing in the kitchen with the lights off. Days where anything everyone says attacks your sensitive, glass-like emotional system which trembles with pain, and it all feels like they see right through you and they think you're "too much." A day where you're so sensitive that when someone moves away just to get a water or a sweater — you're sure it's your awful, see-through energy that you haven't quite figured out how to calm or process that day. Then you wonder if you should even be trusted with such big energy at all, when clearly you're still such a terrible, fallible person. Where the relationship you were over the moon excited about screeches- halfway to the stars- only to make U-turn and rocket calamitously back to earth. And maybe all your excitement over that relationship was one more way to distract you, to deny yourself from your real work- you— so here we are again, back to the way you truly, honestly, treat and see yourself— which is not so great all the time. Certainly better than last year, but abusive pockets- caves and ditches- for sure. It's these days where even your dog seems disappointed in you, she slinks past and around your touch, not wanting anything to do with your clearly funky karma. When, in the car, going back to yoga teacher training for the tenth day or so-feeling peak vulnerable and torn open- you hear a song on the radio achingly similar to your ex fiancés style and voice, and you remember why you fell in love with him in the first place.

You remember his powerful brand of magic that lulled you to him. And you remember those two kids who couldn't stop beaming at each other, because they'd found the secret to life, yes they'd finally found each other. And you are reminded you feel no magic today, and wonder what it ever felt like to have it, and if you lost if for taking it for granted, like you have done with so much in your life. If you burned right through it like everything else. And despite how full your life had been beginning to feel, when you look around and there is only you in the borrowed house, alone, and you can't lie to yourself about that. And on the table is a packet of your old cds you shared with him, with that burned disc that says "to Tim and Sarah," with the heart written by your names, and you still, despite all the other things you've tossed, you just can't bring yourself to toss that. You can't toss it, and you can't listen to it either. And so it remains. Something addressed to the both of you, a unit, a love, that will never ever exist again. And then today when at the end of this incessant reminders of pain and loss, all you just want to slink into the store for a box of macaroni and cheese to be eaten in its entirety in bed, you run into your most recent lover- almost a year ago now it's been, you've been so careful- so overly protective of yourself since he hurt you.

And until seeing him again just like that, in the parking lot, the hurt comes back, and he does that ignoring thing he likes to do, that he does so so well.

Like you never knew him, like you never shared a bed on cold winter nights, like he never padded out to start your car in the frozen morning and make you coffee.You are alone. Maybe it's Goddess Kali, for certainly we invoked her in class.

With these deities it can very much like in Harry Potter- say their name, and here they come. Maybe this is her trail of necessary destruction of what does not serve for re-creation. Maybe this is her tearing down all the illusions with her scythe. Maybe this is like how when my new friend, that new relationship, told me about why they burn all the plant life along the beach path so that when it regrows its stronger and healthier than it was before— fertilized from the ash of the dead life.

Maybe it's in the stars. Maybe it's just a "bad" day for me astrologically. Maybe I'm paying a karmic debt. Maybe I am not embodying tantra because I want out instead of in. I am decidedly still figuring out where to re-enter this real world- or if I even want to, or what, again, the real world even is. I still retreat back into myself at the first sign of danger.

Sometimes I want to tunnel straight into Gaia and sleep inside her, tight in fetal position until it feels safe to come out. Sometimes I look up at the stars and think-or do I know— that out there is home, not here. No, here is just a mission. Oh, but while I'm here, can't I really love? Can't I really be here? Sometimes my Goddess realm is the only realm I feel at home in, it's the only way that makes sense- but even that has been questioned without mercy today. I felt so much excitement in the first week of immersive training, but now the reality that we're coming to a break, and that I'm really back here on the island is sinking in. Yes my soul feels home by the ocean but the social parts, the human parts, of being in the world, are causing me pain. Today a cold voice inside inside me asked "Why do you shove your awakening in people's faces? Why must you always go on and on about it? What if the people who don't believe in awakenings are right? What if everyone thinks I'm evangelical? Oh yeah, and Why don't I just "tone it down?"

Some people tell you keep shining while others say you're too pushy about shining, or don't shine so bright- you give them a headache. I am VERY good at making people uncomfortable. Too weird sexy messy raw honest open. Always. Like a butterfly splayed open and pinned beneath glass. Today I remembered that terrible no good awful feeling I had last spring, right before I fled. (Oh running away, my biggest samscara, what for certain I am here to heal). Here on the island they call new people "washashores." I don't like the term, it suggests so much impermanence, drifting, it speaks of a lost or jettisoned object which strikes me to my core, for I certainly have been one, over and over again. Today, I remembered that impermanent sense I felt last year — that I came in like the tide, and that, as soon as he was done with me, he couldn't wait for me to go out like the tide. A piece of driftwood, homeless forever at the mercy of the waves. When I don't stand in my own fire, I can feel that happening. I can feel myself washing away. And this is suffering. I am suffering, torn apart by what's real and what's not. Torn apart by this world and the one my soul is from. This level of suffering is still very much possible and real- no matter how much I have felt the Divine. I won't deny the pain. I will feel it.

Some days are seamless, all Divinely guided, and some days, like today, had frayed seam upon frayed seam. Today it was all I could do to limp into the borrowed bed hours before the sun itself turned in. Maybe I am under Kali's boot. The excess burning off, the fire leveling me to the ground to rise from ash, healthier and stronger than ever. She's killing off the sick and dying inside of me. For about an hour tonight, I thought maybe I've just finally had enough of this feverish Divine dream, and I'll return to my old ways, to the old life. I'll call a doctor and get a prescription. I'll let him tell me I had a psychotic break with reality, and then I'll get back on prozac and I'll take 2 Xanax a night and sleep until this feverish, white light, white hot wild mystical dream subsides. I'll try normal again until, when I close my eyes the Goddess realm no longer exists, and people stop being so afraid of me. Until I, until I stop being so afraid of me.

I got where I am

by putting

one foot in front

of the other.

[The Butterfly Had to Die

Before She Could Fly.]

Don't forget the butterfly had to crawl, and then she had to die before she could fly. And in between those stages, she had to lie there in the dark cocoon for a while, not sure what the *(&^ was happening to her as everything she knew disappeared. Maybe she was dying. Yes, this was most certainly it, the end...she surrendered. But then... she started changing, thinking new thoughts and seeing new things and she started growing, yes, she started forming small thin wings, and then with the life returning inside of her she just kept beating her new wings against the resistance, and they kept getting bigger, stronger, until one day, she was strong enough to break through the cocoon, the cage, and get free. And then she saw her beautiful dress of silken wings, a downright Nature's Versace, a dress of wings so unique and splendid, one she could never have imagined herself, and she felt the air beneath her as she flew and she could see herself and she loved who she was, how strong and brave and beautifully different, and that her grace and beauty brought others joy. She had needed the resistance to build her strength, she had needed to know dark so she could know light, she needed to know prison so she could know freedom, death to know life, and she needed to crawl so she could know what it was to fly. And then, she realized looking back, what it had all been for. It was all part of the process, part of mother nature's endless cycles of life and death. And if she could have gone back in time she would have told herself, surrender to the now, and trust the process.]

Spring, Martha's Vineyard, 2012.

Only Love is Real.

I got shaken down to my core. I need that once in a while, my beliefs questioned— it only strengthens them. It only strengthens me. All of that was just winds of change blowing through my leaves and taking the dead and the weak ones away. The Awakening is real. I felt shamed for a few days about my Light. It's big. So is yours. But it's confusing when you're walking between old and new paradigms— we are breaking the mold as we enter the new era of Aquarius. You're on brand new territory. You are seeing things no one has ever seen before, only prophesied. I will grow bolder and bolder with my sharings as the days continue, for this is the message I've been given. I don't want you to hide your light, if you are reading this, you are helping heal the world with your light and your heart. No shame for Love. No shame for Beauty. No shame for Compassion. No shame at All. You are healing yourself so you can heal the world. You are undressing from your past and your ancestor's painful pasts and you are headed home. Three weeks ago when I was still in my kitchen in Virginia, crossing to the cupboard for a glass of water, and a force stopped me in my tracks. I get taken into my Goddess Realm very fast, have I told you what it looks like? It's mist-covered land, we're on the grass, open rolling hills stretch out forever and I can feel the sea nearby. There are beautiful, preternaturally beautiful, Goddesses in white surrounding me with long flowing waist-length hair. There are flowers woven in their hair and they have bands of silver and gold around their heads. When I am sourced and settled and I close my eyes, they are waiting for me. There is so much peace and love, but there is also urgency. They caress me, they love me, they groom me, they touch my heart and hair with their beautiful fingers of light. I am one of them, but also their messenger for this plane. They tell me things and then they send me back here when I open my eyes. In the kitchen in Virginia, I felt myself cross my hands over my heart. Then they said "The Angels are Here. The Time Has Begun. You Will Be Called into Service." Some of the things I saw weren't so easy. I don't know how people can watch those multi-million dollar Hollywood blockbusters about Armageddon, when Armageddon is already here for the people of Syria, Rwanda, Afghanistan, Iraq, Libya, and other places all over the planet, they have it rolling through their streets already and have for years. Paying to watch two hours of fear and death when fear and death have gripped our planet already makes me feel so sick. I don't understand it. It hurts to look. The time is here and now to serve the Light. Love has to take the place of fear. Love will if you let it. Send love to your fear. This is important work, and it's real.

Join the Army of Love. "The Angels Are Here. The Time Has Begun. You Will be Called into Service."

The Light is Real. Be one with it. Let it bathe your heart, cleanse your soul, guide you, and shine forth to light the way for others. When in Doubt, Love On Warrior. Love On, Goddess. The healing of self and planet must be awakened in every single heart. Let's save the plants, the animals, the sea, and our children's children. Let's be a planet of Love, Light and Healing. Let this be our Legacy.

This is a touch starved world.

This is a love starved land.

Rise Up Light Workers.

[**The Witch's Hands.** That was the first time I began to remember. Prostrate on the floor/The way my mother had been that early evening in the living room.Cracked open. "Get up ," I cried. "Why would you listen to others when only your heart knows what's true?" Why would we take, any advice but our own?

I didn't know then /When you're cracked open like that/ You're on the operating table/ For Spirit to get its hands in you. And when he left I wanted so badly for a Witch to put her hands inside of me Take out my heart /And put in a new one I prayed for that so much—

And that's exactly what happened. But not before it got much much darker. / Yes just like how night/ gets soupy inky black/ Right Before the dawn breaks. And the witch finally put her hands inside me and alchemized the pain and that witch I remembered in my dreams- Was me. She whispered, "you are coming to save yourself. You are always coming, to save yourself."]

Martha's Vineyard, Spring 2012.

A New Friend.

Yesterday morning Gracie and I sat on the beach with my new man friend as a boat full of women with big friendly smiles rowed up on shore. On the side of the green and white hull the name "Grace" was painted in red. They smiled at us, they patted Gracie's head, she followed them as they walked their oars down the shore, then trotted back to us. She always comes back. Grace always comes back. Why do I ever doubt it? {What is Grace? Love. What is Love? Grace}. I know this but it is not yet embedded in my core. The morning was beautiful, but the day was spent in fear. I am slowly letting that friend, that someone into my life and that small- yet enormous- act has plagued me with panic: yesterday, all day, I recalled my losses in razor sharp detail over my heart, and the fear followed me into my sleep. Although I have been seeded with Anahata- Unconditional Love- something I never would have understood two years ago—I can love the whole world, I can love the Universe, I can love the people who have hurt me- although I can love BIG, I cannot yet love again in the details, the part of me that could love intimately has been hidden away for a year, licking her wounds, swearing off the world. "I will be a lonely warrior," I have told myself. "I will help heal others through the alchemy of my pain, I don't need another's love when I have so much Divine love." In my darkest dreams, I am left, over, and over, and over again. The worst part of these dreams is that they start out that my lover or mother has come back, and my heart soars and I am overcome with joy. "You're back," I say, "Thank God You're back," only for them to leave again- brutally. The lover leaves with disdain, a small brown suitcase in his hand, "you're the same broken girl, you'll never change, what was I thinking," the door slamming behind him. The mother leaves with sorrow, sadness, pulled back to heaven. "I wish I could stay, little one, I love you, I'm so sorry." In the dreams, it's so real. I am always left alone in an empty house, calling out for them, shattered into a million pieces. I hadn't had these dreams in a while, but last night they rolled in like storm clouds, flooded the bedroom. It is a gift of fierce love to see your deepest ears so clearly. It's up to you what you do with this information. I write with tears in my eyes, at the same time I know I am supported by Grace, like the boat that anchored at our feet in the harbor. If I can see the wound, I can heal it. I am grateful to have seen into my soul last night, seen what it fears the most, as painful as the dreams were. So, I'm sorry I didn't write yesterday- sorry for me- this love that flows through me is my life-force, without it, I'm am withered and empty. When I write it down, only then can I see what is happening.

Yesterday was spent curled up in a ball in the five dollar dress I bought at the Hawaiian market hours after they pulled me out of Pele's riptide. It was all I could do to try to understand what I was feeling. Then with sleep, the dreams brought the movies. In the theater, I saw the truth, I saw the saddest movie of my soul. Now I leave the theater, walk into the sunlight of the new day, and begin this new journey of healing the girl left behind. Like a woman at a crossroads, I see the path to take- heal the abandonment, and vow to stop self abandoning, return to the world. I have sequestered myself into my writing and transformation this year, I have kept people at arm's distance- loving them with my whole heart- yet safely in my Divine bubble. The big picture, never the intimate, messy details. This is not Tantra. This is not being here WHILE YOU ARE HERE- ever so briefly.

"Leave the cave," Shakti says. Walk in to the world. When you're keeping your loved ones at bay, you're not really living. When you're doing as I do- only loving them but not letting them love you- it's like living behind one-sided glass. I can see them, but they can't see me. I can give, but I can't receive. This is your mission: RECEIVE LOVE WITHOUT FEAR. Be. Loved.

Be in the world while you have this fleshly body. Let people see your flaws and your fears- your mess. If they leave, they weren't meant to stay. So let what's going to happen, happen. Allow yourself to be loved with the chance of being left. Also allow yourself to be loved with the chance of it being amazing. Either way, what I'm feeling is a fear of change, and change is life. I fear being seen and left. My teacher says, you will always be whole, no matter who is by your side. And despite the pain of my lovers having left me, it was always for the greatest good of my soul. Fear is assuming you have any idea what is going to happen, and haven't I learned- we can't and we don't ever have any idea? And isn't that all part of this big beautiful, scary, awe-inspiring mystery? Didn't I buy a ticket to be here? Didn't life ask for me and didn't I ask for life? Doesn't everything in my being tell me to allow the mystery? To deepen into it? Haven't I been supported this far? Hasn't this last year only led me to greater healing with each step? I wish you, and me, great courage as we allow our mess to be seen by another, without fear, and as we allow our mysteries- the great play of life- to unfold.

[She said, "Darling, I want to make sure/

One thing is Understood/ Always and Only/

Use Your Powers for Good."]

Martha's Vineyard, Spring, 2012.

How Is This Going to End?

"How is this going to play out?" He asked.

Don't you know? I wanted to say. It will end. It will die. It will pass. This is how it all plays out and this is how it all ends, it dies. Sooner or later, this will end.

"Don't resist anything," said the ocean last night. None of it: the darkness or the light. The fear, the pain, or the loss. The beauty, joy, or love. Don't resist any part of your life. Let it all in. When I resist fear I resist love. When I resist pain I resist joy. You cannot have one with out the other. So allow it all. ["I want to feel my life while I'm in it." Meryl Streep]

I don't know about you but most of my pain comes from regret: from not loving or living enough when that thing or person was in the palm of my hands, when it was ripe and alive and ready. I don't want that for you. If you are one of the lucky and blessed enough to have someone you love nearby, Go hold them until your breath synchs up together. Breathe deeply together in silence, then tell them you love them forever, in the flesh for now but forever in spirit.

Had I not tried in vain to stall the seasons of my life. Had I let the river continue to carry me without grasping like a mad woman at the passing shore. Had I only let my fiancé go when he first put his foot out the door. Had I only allowed the information the doctor's gave me: that mom was leaving for Heaven: even as they told me, I denied it, buried in illusion, and eventually caused so much more suffering. Had I not fought so hard to keep my world neat and tidy and the same forever in my tiny ego-mind. Fantasy robs us of reality and the experience of life is why we are here. It's all that devastating, terrified attachment that causes so much suffering. Fear holds on so tight. I didn't love my mother enough in the present. So when she died, I was obsessed with the past, wanting it back so badly, wanting my do-over. I brutalized and chastised myself for years for not loving her enough in the moment. I lived in the past for almost ten years, aching for her back so I could show her how much I loved her. That's what causes so much pain, that ugly black-tar remorse. Love now, not later. Love now fully, there is no later. Don't resist the information you are given. Don't resist your mortality, own it. Allow the truth to settle into your bones and make you wiser, stronger, and more alive. Don't be afraid that we die and everything else does too, let it embolden you, let it enliven and awaken you.

I wish for you to enter each experience knowing it is fleeting. I wish for you to hold each person and animal knowing they will die. To know it will die- Gracie, me, Dad, my sister, my loved ones- is to really love them while they are here. I wish for you to love it and live it with all your heart while it's there, while its heart beats, the relationship, the person, the moment.

Stay present, stay present, stay present. [Stay with me. Love, The Present]. If you are fearful, you are in the future, you are not here in the moment. Your longing for the past and your fear of future change will break your heart. You can only love now, you can only live now. It may seem like a curse but it's actually a blessing. Look around: everything in your life right now is only for a flickering moment. The good and the bad, love it all. Gather up your loved ones before time takes them away. Gather up your loved ones before the earth gathers them back. Gather up your life and act in it before it's a dream, a desire, before it's only a memory. Don't be fooled: we know how all of this will end. In dust, in memories. I see time's marks on my face, I know where this fleshly body is eventually headed, back into the ground. And it's the most powerful information one can process, that it all passes, and so do you.

That the end is coming is definite and real. But here's the real mystery and the real adventure: Now what? What will you do with it while you have it and you're here? Here's what I know: You can do absolutely anything you want with it. Anything.

You can do anything you want. Choice is your greatest weapon, your greatest power. Choose love. Choose life, choose your life, choose you, choose Now, Choose your dreams.

So for now I am here, allowing my life and the full extent of the earthly experience. Wherever the tides take me. That is my promise to this life. I already know, whether it's tomorrow or in fifty years, this will end in loss. So I love now, so that I may let it go with grace when the time comes, without regret. This is where enlightenment meets earthly love. This is my answer for now, love now, so I may one day let it go with grace. So that one day I myself may go with grace.

This life is a bridge we walk that disappears behind us with each step. If you try to reach behind yourself, you will fall. We are only fully supported in the moment.

If there is one thing I know it's that nothing has killed me yet. That I have a fleshy body but an indestructible, infinite, ancient spirit. I am built for storms. I can handle loss. I can let you go. I invite the unknown. I can love in the now. Don't lie to yourself: you know how this thing ends: and that's that it does, indeed, end.

[The World Needs It

and You're the One to Do It.

And when you know what you have to do you have to do it

You know you have to do what you know you have to do

Don't Tell Them. Show Them.]

Martha's Vineyard, Spring, 2012.

Grateful for the Work.

In the late spring, the kind of weather where the sweater ends up around your waist by noon, I was in my healer's house, on a road in West Tisbury called Music Street. I hear that music, like a happy, carefree piano, when I bike down that broadly paved and leafy street between an old gray general store and a white wooden church. Farther down it turns into a bumpy sand road that opens up to fields, and it's always struck by gallons of light. I was going to her a lot for long talks. I could cry to her, I could play Scrabble with her in the kitchen while the tea steeped, I could always, always ask her for help. Real help. On the tree outside her cottage, she tied shells to the branches. In the light breeze, they clink together and shine.

Anyway, as she knew, I had been doing so much work. We had started together, she had saved my life. All that hard work, like how Marianne Williamson says, "Spiritual progress is like detoxification. Things have to come up in order to be released. Once we have asked to be healed, then our unhealed places are forced to the surface." I was working so hard on all the ghosts rising to the surface, working on my alchemy, to turn the rotted parts of my heart into gold. To turn my old thought patterns, grief, self-torture, guilt, shame, into cleansings truths like forgiveness, compassion, mindfulness and love. I was reading the books in the bathtub, cleaning my body while I cleaned my head and heart, watching my life change in the air around me. Physically I was doing the holy work of chores, outside, with the animals. Lifting and shoveling and sweeping, and I was grateful for the work.

The work was working, my life was changing, but I was exhausted. That spring day I was in such limbo. Spiritually, I felt stretched out over a canyon, one foot on the crumbling old and familiar, the other foot reaching out to the unknown, the previously impossible. Of course, she could see this, but I was trying to describe it anyway as we were sitting by the fire eating chocolates. I was missing my old love, I was longing for my new love. Mid-leap into my new life, the crash and burn of a love affair sent me spiraling back to the ground. The old me was fighting for the reigns, she wanted to give up and be swallowed by bleak, self-indulgent, endless despair, free to feel and be terrible. The new me wanted to be released from the suffering, and walks as love, and she knew, she knew how. But KNOWING and DOING is the crossroads. I was caught at a crossroads, my test had begun. Was I ready to embody all this accrued wisdom, to step into timelessness, the present moment, forgive and be set free?

"Why aren't you just there yet?" she asked in her uniquely candid manner.

"You could be there if you really wanted. You're the only thing holding yourself back."

A shock of resonation flashed through me, that shock of truth.

"There's nothing left for you back there. It's done," she said. "Why are you trying to hold on to it?"

"Fuck it," she said. "Fuck all that pain. Take the leap."

[You are Ready. Become].

[She Said, "I Pity the Woman,

Who Doesn't Use Her Gift."

He said, "I Pity the Man,

Who Doesn't Share His Gold."

And George Bailey said, "The Only Thing

We Can Take With Us is What We Give Away."]

Martha's Vineyard, 2012.

Seeing Butterflies.

In late winter in Virginia, my mother's friend and I were sitting in front of the fire eating dinner and sharing a bottle of red wine. She was telling me about her daughter who was going through a hard time, her whole life had been pulled out from under her.

"But— " she said, pointing at me— "she keeps seeing butterflies."

"That's wonderful," I said.

"Well what do you think that means?" she asked me.

"Well, what does she think it means?" I said.

"She…she thinks it could be signs that she is going to break out of her cocoon and fly."

"Well, then that's exactly what it means," I said.

"Good," said my friend, nodding. "Good."

This morning on my way to my friend's house I stopped at the general store, and the manager and I smiled at each other when we passed by.

"You're feeling better, huh?" he asked.

"Gotta get down to get up," I said.

"Ain't that always the way," he laughed.

Do you know what a StarSeed is? That is what you very well could be. You could have gone through all of your extended and constant suffering in the first part of your life only to wake up at a predestined time— somewhere between 2006 and now to assist the new earth in its awakening. Your long-storied and diverse experiences of suffering have enabled your deep understanding and compassion for those who still sleep and suffer. It will only deepen your compassion for the humans you serve. You only want to help. You only want to serve. You only want to save the world. What you are is a lightworker. You know the light is real because you have lived in and survived the dark. If you're still processing the dark and your life is still falling apart, know it's about to end, and that you can and will heal and wake up over night. Just keep doing the work. You are healing so that you may heal others.

Last night as I closed the door to the cabin I stopped and looked up one more time at that glowing blue moon. It beamed, pulsated with its light and seemed to say, "Know This. You are deeply, deeply loved. The energies of the light are working through you. Carry on with your mission." Just then, a star shot down across the black outline of the trees.

[TOUCH EVERYTHING THAT WAY.

She said, "Something strange and beautiful is happening inside of me / I can hear the thoughts of the birds I can hear the songs of the trees /I can feel the heartbeat of the beasts / I can live in each moment like it's my very last feast/ My heart is the moon/ My tears are the sea/ Today I touched everything in the world/ Like it was my lover/ I touched everything that way

Including me."]

[AN OPEN HEART. An open heart means that what wants to leave may leave. What wants to come may come. And what wants to stay may stay. Keep it open. And love will find a way.]

Martha's Vineyard, Spring, 2012.

A Channeling.

Dear You,

It does not matter what we think,

what we say, what we do.

We are lost and dying, following each other deeper

into the abyss.

We need stars like you to lead us out of the darkness, so please do not listen to

our fear when you begin to break free.

KEEP GOING.

The only thing that ever mattered was the voice

in your heart- not the cries of the herd.

This is your moment, you are our Hope.

Ignore us to save us.

Blaze a trail of light so that we might follow.

Liberate yourself so that you might liberate us all.

Love,

The Masses

[She said a soft being/ Is a receptive being / And to receive the gifts of this life / You have to be so so open/ Totally untethered to the future or the past/ Live this moment like it's your first and last/ Your hands have to be open/ Your mind has to be open / Your heart has to be open/ Open it up even more/ Open it up 'till it's sore/ You can't hold on / to what is gone/ Softer now / And softer still/ Every cell opens up to receive the new / To be what's true/ Allow yourself to be even more/ You/ You have to be so open / to Love from God/ from the Great Mother/ and to and from The Other/ Softer now/ And softer still/ Let your neck fall back/ like a lamb to love's slaughter/ You're safe/ God loves you / you're his daughter/ Open up / Go limp/ Be like the lips of a pitcher/ Receiving cool holy water/ Drink the air like win/ Remember everything is always fine/ Trust/ like a dog offers its soft under belly / to the hands of a stranger/ Like the baby turkey waddled up to you in the woods/ As if you were its mother/ Holy loving vulnerability/ As if every moment you were whispering /"Dear life, I trust you with my life."/ For what other way is there / But to love/ Totally bare/ Go slow now/ You're in the flow/ Look around / you want to remember/ Everything / And don't forget to breathe and sing/ the way water does/ as it falls over its edge/ Into the ever-waiting and loving pond/ of the great beyond/ When it lets go thats when it sings its greatest song/ What doesn't love me/ I allow to be taken from me/ As I dive to swim again/ in Love's great sea.]

Martha's Vineyard, Spring, 2012.

Being There.

I know where my dangerous dream-like state started. Not my dream state where I connect with the Divine- that's hardly a dream anymore—it's the where I go when I do not choose presence. It started at 12 when my parents split and I didn't want/couldn't handle the reality. Then she got sick, Mom got really sick, and they said she might not make it, and that was clear, with how bad things got, how much she deteriorated, the hair loss the hospital stays and the seizures. So I started no longer "being there" in a room with pain. It wasn't convenient, it wasn't pretty, and it hurt like hell. When I couldn't physically run away I was mentally running.

And then she died and my own soul retreated, it didn't want to be down here in this earthly body with all this pain and that's when I started sleepwalking, and later learned to numb pain with alcohol and pills. That's when I started my physical running. Boys, jobs, apartments, state-hopping, burning all those bridges, blazing a trail of fear.

Now Gracie has Lyme, she's so weak she falls over when she tries to stand and it hurts to watch. So now when it hurts, I listen, and I stay in my body. I say, "I'm not going anywhere." No mental escape. My discomfort is my trigger- pay attention, stay with it. Stay in my body, stay in my soul, stay in my heart.

I am practicing really being with her in her pain. I am not going somewhere else in my mind or allowing myself to retreat. She can feel my soul's presence, not just bodily presence. Remember, Animals and Children are energy readers. That is their language.

When I touch her I am not thinking about something else. I am simply with her. "I am Right Here." What a huge fucking difference. I hold her and wish I had held my mother this way but I was a teenager, and God Dammit I have to forgive myself, I know she has forgiven me.

But I did this, I have retreated, since I was young, I am here, but not here. And haven't you felt the pain of someone who was there but not there, and like you were shouting into a vacuum, their lack of presence in their body, in the moment, making you feel even more alone? You could touch them but it doesn't really touch them.

I think of the earthly angels, nurses, in hospitals and all the unsung caregivers who tend to others, physically, all day and every day. When I am alone and I feel The Presence, when I feel the angel wings wrap around me, I know caring for others in their time of need is the holiest of work. reiki, reiki, reiki, it's time for my reiki practice again. I don't just want to reach you through these flat thin screens, I want to physically touch others while I can. The sense of touch in this earthly body heals.

There is a magic energy coursing through us. We don't know this yet enough in our culture because as my first reiki master Libby Barnett teaches, "this is a touch-starved world." But I knew, yesterday, that the prescription for this earth is not pills or war but Love. I wish I could write everyone a prescription for deep, healing, stay-with-you-through-the-pain Love, and that it would be Filled.

I have felt the deep remorseful pain of turning away from someone I loved who needed me. I will never ever do this again. I am not running away. I am staying in the fire. Mine and yours. The holiest of work is to love another, and sit with them, fully present, in their hour of need. To not turn away. There comes that holy point in everyone's life when they say, "I could no longer look away."

The veil is so thin right now. I barely close my eyes and the messages rush through. Be like the angels, and be with others in their pain. This is the message. I feel my armor being worked on, I feel there will be battles- more. I feel I am learning the lessons of the warrior, and I am learning not to be afraid. I will stand in your fires with you. And I don't want to think on it anymore. I want to act on it. The time is now, the angels say, for Action. It's certainly not that imaginary time, "later."

The time is now to Show Up for others. Make a decision- go with your first one, your gut one, and don't turn around. Never ignore your gut.

You know what to do and you know how to do it. Stop Hiding. Stop Retreating. Stop rehearsing. Stop Being Halfway in and Halfway Out. Show Up. Show Up. Show Up. Open hearted. Then Keep Going, and Keep Showing Up. Action. Action is for the earthly body, for this incarnation. Only in the present can we Act. Show Up, Show Up, Show Up. This is how it works. Show Up, Show Up, Show Up, in this lifetime, in this moment, in this now, Show Up. Really BE. Follow the intuition at every turn, the inner yellow brick road. Be in your body. Be in your heart. Be with you. Be with them.

Be of service. Get messy. Get your hands dirty, roll up your sleeves and tuck up your skirt and GET IN THERE. You know how took love yourself, you know how to care for yourself, and that was preparation for this part. It's time to be of assistance. It's time to be of care. It's time to be of service. There is nothing more than this, than to love and to help others in their times of need. Nothing more to this, no other secret, than to love others. That's it. That's the whole damn thing. Love. Get out there or get in there, and get to work with your Love. You will never be more ready than now to Love. There is no better or more dire time, it will never be more needed, than now, to Love. Love Now. There is no Later. While I was here, I want to be able to say, that I was really *here*.

[If only we searched inside ourselves/ As deeply as we searched The Internet.]

Martha's Vineyard, Spring, 2012.

Omens.

I'm thinking of these times of change as corridors and bridges to my next evolution, maybe it helps you too- thinking of change as a bridge. It does feel like I'm fumbling down a dark hallway, not quite sure where I'll end up- the instinct continues to be that everything's going to be alright, I can feel the light I just can't see it.

Sunday I rushed to the beach- I had really been looking forward to a moment with my book in the sun— and it was after a morning where I had been thinking about male and female relationships so much, and how we're re-aligning after so much imbalance, and I had allowed myself to be angry, which I never really do anymore.

So I was sort of on guard and uncertain about feeling anger, and even though I wrote out a lot of that frustration in here I still had it on the beach. And I had only gotten to the top of the path when Gracie started seeming stiff in her legs, and we barely made it onto the sand before she wanted to stop walking. I was worried about her and tense, and I had just pulled out my towel when I looked up and saw a beautiful seal washed up near us in the surf- and she (she looked like a she) was dead. Newly. And so beautiful, not a mark on her, big black eyes, long wet whiskers, folded flippers, the dogs of the sea.

Gracie and I walked around her to make sure she wasn't alive, and then we sat back on the towel and I just watched for a moment. All plans to relax were abandoned. It was only a few minutes later I saw another seal's head at a distance bobbing frantically through the water toward her.

This one (a he?) swam up to the surf in front of me and stopped, locking eyes with me and afraid of Gracie, who was perplexed by the whole scene. Then, even in his fear of us, he pushed over to the beached seal and waddled around her, worried and attentive, and he was prodding her with his nose and then he pushed her back into the water with his slick head and began swimming around her, prodding her more to move again- and every time she got swept to the sand he got behind her and pushed her back in the water, then tried to keep her up and swimming again and he did this for forty five minutes, I know, because I sat there bawling the whole time. Just me, Gracie, and those two seals, one dead one living and not a soul else on the beach.

He could have actually done this for longer after I left but I couldn't watch anymore, I finally had to finally get up and go home. But I watched for as long as I could, just sobbing and saying, "I am so so sorry," to the seal who wanted so desperately to bring the other one back to life. And for part of it the old wall came up— I really wanted it to stop and I wanted it to be over and NOT HAPPENING. But it was, it was happening. This is, this right now, this is happening.

"Stay with it," Nature said, "stay with it, witness it," and I did, but it was torture, like my heart was being ripped open. "Stay with it." Do as nature does, keep listening to the patterns and the behaviors of Nature, the highest wisdom, the wisdom of the feminine- this is how we return to the earth and unlock secrets to life - and I watched how this seal ran to another's pain and didn't turn away from it. And the instinct- the fearless fight for precious life that was ignited in him- for another's life, a stranger, a mate, a sibling, a child, I don't know. But I know this is part of my path, to be able to sit with death and sickness and pain.

I know us humans run from our pain and other's pain. I know animals, always in the present moment, do not do this. And even though we think we don't, I also know we build walls and run from love. And what's life without pain and what's life without love?

I was meant to watch those seals and see one not only move toward another's pain but toward it fearlessly and with devotion. His lessons had me staying with my own pain and that of others all week. Moving toward, not away. And I still feel my pain, and

Gracie still feels some of her pain, but we're still sitting with it. I knew things would be hard for a while and they have been, the days laced heavily with sadness, Gracie with her Lyme, me with my new upheaval and all my unknowns, and I'm leaving this cabin I love so much and that has healed me so much. I love this cabin in the woods, I miss it as I sit in it.

But when I am not afraid of pain, what am I afraid of? Nothing.

I can sit with my pain, I can sit with your pain. I am being asked to make changes once again, and to be stronger yet. I don't want to keep moving around, I have been praying to stay in one place. To make this life sustainable and grounded. But I'm being asked to shake it up change and transform— again? I ask— "Yes," I hear, "Again. Change is your only constant." And I'm seeing spiders everywhere- so are some of my friends- and the more you see the more change is on its way. See how they build a majestic web one day, only to tear it down that night, and start over the next day, such faith in their endless power to create.

There are only two directions, onward and upward. I'm in the spaces in between. I'm in the fuzz, the hallways, the transitions. And I'm staying with it, I'm walking through the dark being lead by the light in my heart. When I'm in the darkness, it becomes clear to me that fear just creates more darkness, but love turns on the light and illuminates possibilities. So I live with the questions and I choose love and I move forward, today that is all I can do, and most days this is all that is ever really asked of us.

[She said she could hear his footsteps getting closer with each beat of her heart / she said she could feel his coming/ like a buck on a moonless night/ like wind on the water/ a feeling as clear as the steer/ of an oar/ like when her moon time came/ And her womb ached with a knowing/ A woman's full bodied knowing/ as sure as any compass/ as clear as any crystal/ as north as any star/ as true as any blue/ Where have you been she asked and he said *I've been preparing for you*.]

Summer, 2012, Martha's Vineyard

Makeover Movies.

I'm finding myself inspired by other women transforming in front of my eyes and I'm reminded this change is VERY real.

This is why I have always loved makeover movies so much: you see the heroine walk in one door as her old self and come out another one as her new self. This is why I loved the woman escaping to nature movies so much, Baby Boom, Practical Magic, women throwing themselves into the wild to see what they're made of. Somewhere I knew this was possible, I think that's why I was so drawn to transformation movies, I knew mine was coming, some day. I'm always writing these sorts of movies in my head, and actually living them on the physical plane- well, since my last shipwreck when I had to choose a new life for myself. I chose the woman goes to the country and finds herself life. I chose the makeover movie. I took the Anais Nin path of "If I hadn't created my own world I would surely have died in other peoples."

I remember when I started hearing people speaking aloud their New Thoughts, or maybe I was just finally hearing them.. I drove to the dentist in February on a snowy day in Virginia and he had his tools in my mouth and he started to talk about pain, just the physical kind, and he was talking about how afraid his patients were of it, and then he stopped, "you know, people are so afraid of pain, any kind," he said. Then he took the tool out of my mouth and he said, "They're so afraid of feeling... anything." I watched him process this, that we're all so afraid to feel our feelings, and I just nodded away there was nothing to say.

My friend Christine said last night, that "fear is the belief that we are ever separate from God." I remember reading that at Kripalu last year, this time exactly last year, sitting by the window in the cafe over looking the courtyard, writing a friend in Omaha, that I was awakening to the Witch in me, explaining what that was, the alignment with nature.

It was around the time someone told me God was the ocean and we were all drops in the water, I mean I really was starting to feel A PART OF IT ALL, and it was thrilling. But I'd fled to Kripalu because it was the only place that made sense for me to go, my awakening was so total and abrupt, the only person I could really talk to about it was my aunt Amy, otherwise I was sure I'd get committed somewhere.

Meanwhile, if anything, I should have been committed the year before, when I was downing a bottle of wine every night on a handful of Xanax. But people do that a lot more than they talk about love and light. People are in fear a lot more than love.

I remember I was all packed up for Kripalu and I was going and I didn't know how long I would be gone for. So we were standing in the driveway and she looked at me like she saw, not a ghost, but an angel. "You look like a completely different person," said a woman who had gazed upon my face her whole life. "I know," I said, my voice shaking, "it's scary." Because I really really did. My hair- which had started to fall out after Tim left, had fluffed out to a totally new texture soft and cloud-like, and it grew longer rapidly, and my skin had began to glow, my body became sinewy and strong. All I can say is I didn't recognize myself, like an ethereal spirit had possessed me. You know how they say "He sold his soul to the Devil," well I felt I'd sold mine to the angels. "You're going to be ok," Amy said as we lingered in the driveway. And then I started to cry - the way I did when I was first waking up, huge, full body, dam breaking heaving sobs. I mean, I was feeling things for the first time in YEARS. I was sobbing out lifetimes of pain. "I'll be ok," I choked. And then I said, much to both of our amazement: "I'm doing God's work." We were both taken aback my the words that came out of my mouth and I certainly did not know they were coming. I didn't form them in my brain first, just a vessel for them. And she just held me, because it was all so very new and strange, for a previously depressed, pill addicted rock journalist to be talking about being a hand for God and rushing off to a spiritual center- to live.

Five hours later I got to that red barn a mile down the road from Kripalu, that just seemed to be open and waiting for me, and Gracie and I just sat there on the steps and I closed my eyes. I was so afraid. I had really "dropped out" of society and had no plan, knew no one there, I just knew I had had what I thought was an Awakening, and like having a child, birthing and raising a new soul takes everything you have.

You have to learn how to feed it, nourish it, grow it. And you can never go back to "how things were" before you discovered your soul. I was sitting on the porch, leaning against the glass doors, and just like the time I felt myself, trance-like, write "lightworker" on my arm, before knowing what that word was or what was happening, I opened my eyes on that porch to see the words "God is Here" scrawled in the dust on the glass of the door of this rented cabin. And it hadn't been there, it hadn't been there before I sat down. A beautiful blond yogini in Omaha asked me how I believed this stuff, that I'm a goddess, that Spirit is real, that we're eternal, that I've lived before. Those messages, I'd say. All of last year, really, is why. What happened to me is why.

I was walking Gracie in the woods this morning and I had a flashback, a flash of an image that I was in the forest surrounded by wild animals, kneeling by a wolf, and while I welcomed the vision I also thought, "it doesn't really matter NOW that I was once a goddess in another life or several. All that matters is I am a goddess in this life, and what will I do with it?" Not to dismiss the realm or my discovery of it, but to make the most of it now, is what I want to know.

'Teach ritual to heal the earth,' said a healer I asked last week, that was the answer she got from Spirit, that to her was my calling. In that cabin in the Berkshires, I remember thinking this spiritual life was going to be so lonely, because at first it was so, so, so, lonely, but that at least I wasn't so alone in a room full of people anymore. But REALLY it isn't lonely and it doesn't have to be, I've attracted a lot of people like me, strong women with big things happening inside of them. We don't have to, nor are we meant to, do this alone. There is of course the cocoon time, before your grow your wings. And the cocoon is dark and isolated for a reason, you have to find your own light and your own self before you re-join the world.

It's good to know what you're healing. It's good to know the dragon you're slaying or the curse you're reversing on your great heroic journey. If I was writing a fable for all of us I would say we all live in a land that Once Upon a Time, during the Fall of the

Goddess, was cursed with a dark spell. It was then that we fell under the illusion we were all separate from each other and nature, we would fall under the illusion that love was outside of ourselves and something we had to seek and earn. There is only one way to reverse the curse, and that is for each one of ourselves to discover and love ourselves. When we love ourselves, we love each other. When we heal ourselves, we heal each other. When we love and heal each other, we love and heal the earth. Rise up against the darkness that fell over the land. Reverse the curse and let love rule. "I heal myself to heal the world."

[You have nothing better to do than live your dream, your dream is your purpose and your purpose serves the world.]

Summer, 2012. Martha's Vineyard.

Walking in the Woods.

There's a way to use all my Authority Issues for good. I mean I have them BIG time. It was a huge part of my suffering in my old life, I couldn't follow the orders of teachers or bosses. I always had to do it my way, be in my own world, I didn't understand one person giving another orders. I was always the Norma Rae, whistle blowing, standing up for other co-workers, breaking the rules, coming in late, leaving on whims. Once I lied to my boss I was sick, and flew to New Orleans to interview Duran Duran in a limbo that rambled around the city. I almost got away with it until I answered his call in the airport bathroom and they called my flight on the speaker. "Where the hell are you?" he asked. I still can't believe he didn't fire me. I'm still grateful for his forgiveness.

I thought, well why don't I employ that rebellion with my Fear, when it's ruling? Why don't I talk back to those shitty fearful voices in my head? Why don't I say to fear, "Oh, yeah? You think I can't rise and walk through that? You think I can't deal with my finances, or be totally honest, or ask them for what I really want, or tell him No..." WHATEVER it is. Challenge Authority, Challenge the authority of your fear. On the other side of your fear, Freedom.

Martha's Vineyard, Summer, 2012.

When Your Path Reappears Beneath Your Feet.

I had an unfortunate run in with maggots recently, they were in something I picked up and I dropped them with that gasp when something that reeks of death. I couldn't help but see them working at my body when I'm placed back in mother earth.

Sunday night I went down to the tourist strip and I saw Pandora, my little ten year old ancient sage friend with long thin legs and a shiny sheet of blond hair, dance under the lights to Donna Summer, I sat crossed legged on the wooden floor in my silk slip I pretend is a dress, Pandora's sweet, olive-skinned fourteen year old sister slumped on one side of me and her mother on the other, a woman who is my mirror image in a lot of ways, someone I'm actually letting know me, because she is a reflection of me, so I don't have to explain that much.

I'm not out much, because the night used to get me into so much trouble. But being out felt really good, there is this whole vibrant world that unfolds when I'm pulling the covers up. As the night went on we watched each dancer steal a moment of immortality in this great mortal play, tick tock, tick tock, and I started thinking about Glory.

What it is, when someone has it for a moment. I think about how many moments I've been blessed with since I woke up. There was something quite unusual, a beautiful, fit, 60 year old woman who moved slowly in white to a recording of a man talking about a piece of music he wrote about death, it played in the background, sometimes you could hear angels sing, but mostly you could hear a pin drop as we watched this woman move to a musing on death. It was great art because it made the audience uncomfortable and if it's making you uncomfortable you have to ask WHY and then you are blessed with great information about yourself. I appreciate the kind of person who is not here to make you COMFORTABLE, she is hear to wake you up. "She's not doing something I recognize. She's not making me 'happy. This isn't familiar.' She's MAKING me FEEL SOMETHING." She was bringing her fear out into the light and watching it dissolve. We were honored guests. At one point she became a Sorceress, so divinely connected to source, her body moving in prayer.

My friend nudged me, "what did you think about her?" she asked, I could tell she dug it by the look in her eyes.

"You could tell she's a survivor," I said. "Only survivors have that kind of courage." My friend nodded.

[She said the lessons are in the fire, they make us richer, they make us wiser.]

This woman had walked through it, and now she was on the other side. You can tell someone who is on the Other Side of life, she's walked through her Great Fire. Phoenix style. She knew life, she had faced death. She knew Glory, she had more than tasted it, it had embraced her and she had become it, she was Glorious.

And when I had a moment of fear and dullness this morning I heard that Great Gatsby line, "All I kept thinking about, over and over, was 'You can't live forever; you can't live forever." And I think about Wayne Dyer, saying, "You have an endless stream of green lights before you." It's true. I know this, I woke up knowing it today. I had wanted to stay in that Sunday night, to eat too much to sleep too early. And I gasp in my throat thinking about missing that moment.

My favorite moments are when someone realizes they have just had ENOUGH of whatever it is that shackles them, the suffering the sickness the fear the oppression, and they finally walk away or through and then, like a river running through their whole body, they can feel their REAL LIFE BEGINNING Again. The path reappears beneath their feet and life is an adventure again. My favorite moments are when people get free.

glo·ry [glawr-ee, glohr-ee]

noun, plural glo·ries,

resplendent beauty or magnificence: "the glory of autumn."

a state of great splendor, magnificence, or prosperity.

["Don't Rush This," she said. "Rush. Nothing. Blow them away with your Grace."]

Summer, 2012, Martha's Vineyard

I Could Feel Him I Just Couldn't See Him.

The only thing that intimidated the last man I dated— that I could tell, at least, I think there were a lot of things unsaid— was my music background, the whole rock n roll girl identity I once had, which I am now learning i must let go of gracefully instead of what I was trying to do- simply say I no longer was her and denounce her. Cast her out the way Im so afraid of being cast out, rejected, never belonging. That doesn't work. To do that same thing to yourself that's been done to you. To abandon yourself the way you've been abandoned. But that way of life served a purpose, fulfilled a dream even, and I should show that girl who lived backstage and chugged red wine and found worth through the men, I should show her love, I should take her to my breast.

Anyway, the radio was playing an alternative rock song in the spring in front of the fire and he guessed correctly I knew the singer personally. "Must be weird turning on the radio and never knowing if someone you know will be singing," he said, and by that he meant men I had "dated." It was things like that that made me think we could work, because without telling him the details he knew what my life was like, he took deeply accurate guesses that made me feel understood. There was a time when I couldn't turn on the radio or flip through a SPIN or Rolling Stone without hearing or seeing a man I once knew. And then I couldn't listen to music for the whole year after my fiancé ended it. So many people I've talked to about broken hearts, they'd said that they couldn't even hear the music they loved for a very long time, their raw heart no match for a song they listened to when they were in love.

But- I was never worried about hearing him on the radio, not that he isn't talented enough, he just doesn't do top 40. And then yesterday I was in my favorite bakery yesterday headed to Sepiessa point, I had called in my egg sandwich and was waiting in a fifteen person line to pay, we were all sort of packed in there, it's a tiny little place. I was already feeling a little panicky with all the people jostling each other about and stepping on flip-flops when a familiar beat started playing in the warm little room. Before I knew it my mouth had gone dry, my hands were shaking, I was sweating a little. It was his voice, it was a song I had heard him sing 300 times on the side of the stage, in the dark. Him in the light, me in the dark. I wanted to bolt, it wasn't just his voice, it was his soul, he really does pour his soul out. That's what art is, right? Your soul?

The girl behind the counter was talking to me but I could only see her lips moving, I was listening so closely, my ears sifting through the other noises in the room. The creeping piano part came and the notes ran up my spine and hit every vertebrae, like the music had me in its claws, its clutches. I could feel him, I just couldn't see him, and the free fall into black feeling is that I know I never will again. The place was too crowded and I was so close to the counter that I waited it out, my heart banging in my chest. It was the first time I had heard his voice in almost 3 years. It feels like a lifetime and it feels like a day.

But these days I have the feeling of a tightrope walker, more than halfway across the way. Of a swimmer crossing a great channel, of holding my breath till I get the other side. If I don't look down, if I don't get distracted, if I don't get scared, if I don't doubt or elude myself into unworthiness or separation, If I stay on my path, I just might make it this time.

[JOAN OF ARC THIS SHIT. She looked around at all the strife. Everything she'd been afraid of her whole life/ Confrontation and the Gossip/ The stones they threw / Her flickering flame of self worth that lied/ "Love and happiness will never come true/ And life is supposed to be tough/ And you'll never be enough"/ At her fear of failure and making choices/ And what they would say, if she did it her way

The way that called inside her soul/ The path of her full truth that would make her whole/ And any other day/ She might had hid cried or thrown a child's fit / But no, she said, those days are forever gone/ Today and from now on/ I'm going to Joan of Arc this shit."]

Martha's Vineyard, Late Summer, 2012.

Missing the Brass Ring.

So I went out to dinner with that man I used to date last night because I want to heal wounds and be mature and not blow up every bridge with men I dated or anyone else in my experience/life. The more conscious we become the more we understand that behavior like that- holding grudges, anger, blame, hate even, aren't in alignment with love. Because we are love, everything that isn't love feels "wrong."

A friend of mine from Virginia texted while we were out, and I told her who I was with and she said, "So you don't burn bridges like me," but I have burned a ton of bridges, I told my friend, ones I wished dearly that I'd kept, even if I couldn't walk it the way I once did, I didn't have to torch it forevermore. Forever is a really long sad time when it means never talking to someone you loved ever again. I told her how I've not only burned bridges I should have kept, I've stormed the castle, set flame to everything in site. As soon as the rejection or betrayal happened I was like Drew Barrymore in Firestarter. SO Proud. SO hot-headed. SO victimized. We are each walking bodies of energy, and we can start an energy storm- dark or light- where every where, where ever we go, Our choice. Fear or Love.

Anyway, so last night was mature but hard, I wanted to lean into him sometimes the way it used to be so easy, but I didn't let myself, I kept the wall up. And there was a time or two he was laughing and would lean to rest his head on mine but I froze up, still protective of myself. Our knees touched at times only because he's so tall and we were folded into a tiny bar top table. We ate at this little tourist dive on the strip and a blind man played piano right next to our table and it added to the melancholy of dinner with an old lover, and my heart was dove-tailing at the diligence and love of the seeing eye dog curled by the singer's side and he was singing Otis Redding, lovelorn Otis Redding. And his silver-haired old friend in a dinner jacket showed up and sang deep baritone harmonies and sipped a glass of red wine.

It was nice, there were moments where we were in sync and on the same page and moments we weren't. The chemistry wasn't there the way it was when I could show him affection with abandon, just a dull ache from me, I think, I think I was the only one aching. There was this moment too, where he started to ask about a mystical-looking ring around my neck and I started to tell him the story, but I said, "do you really want to know," and then he decided he really didn't- "no," he said, shaking his head, laughing me off.

We sort of threw a few passive jabs at each other, which doesn't feel good, really, he definitely thinks my Goddess devotion is flaky and "not realistic." That's probably the thing that made me hurt the most, but anything that makes you question your beliefs is good because I find it ultimately strengthens them, having to re-examine them from time to time: are they still true to you?

But then as soon as I started to really relax and allow myself to enjoy the time, he looked down at his phone, said, "Oh we gotta go," then he straightened his back, signaled the waitress and as we crossed the floor, and the blind man called goodbye to us in between versus. He felt us leaving, his energetic senses so heightened, "good night," we called in return, and it felt so good to do something again in unison.

Idling in my road we hugged goodbye, and I went in and got in bed and had to tell myself that someday I will meet someone who understands me completely, and loves me like shout-it-on-the-rooftops love, for who I am, not who I might be someday or who I once was. Not just for weekends or winter or stay-in-nights, either. The whole real deal again. I'll feel one day the way I felt six years ago when I met my fiancé in an Alphabet City Bar. Crash Bang Boom, done. Your whole life changed in one night.

Up until the sun rose, just holding hands and kissing, under a window in the moonlight, planning our whole lives together. ["We'll get a dog." "No, we'll start with a cat." "Both." "Ok." "And a truck-" "Yes! I've always wanted a truck!" "We'll move downtown. A big apartment by the river." "Wow, my dream is your dream."] I'll feel that again.

Me and this man, last night, we rode the carousel by the sea, the old flying horses, we went round and round together, going nowhere, getting nowhere in the air, and the creepy cranky old carnival music was playing, it was chilly, my cheeks were pink, and he had a tiny little girl in a pink tutu next to him and I was on a horse next to her warm and friendly mother, and we were reaching for the rings, you know the whole point is to get the brass one.

And my friend, I'll call him, was adamant to get it, he was pulling 3-4 rings at one time with his long gangly arms. He's competitive. An Aries. Needs to own, win. It was hard enough for me to grab even one, but I managed to get one every time around. And finally, there it was, waiting for me at my turn, there was the brass ring. I got so excited, I couldn't believe it, I cried out in joy, and then it just slipped through my fingers.

I don't know why I'm stuck on that moment but I am, it's on an endless loop. Just missing the brass ring. The source of pain I've carried since the beginning, is that I don't finish things. I'm all talk, all promise. No delivery. People lose hope in me. I woke up with the ring slipping through my hands, that tiny terrible movie, playing over and over again in my head. It reminded me too much of all the promise I've felt and pressure I've felt for my potential in this life so far, that I can get so close to the brass ring but never quite grab it, like my wedding ring. I got so close to marrying a man I deeply loved. I got so close to having a family. I got so close to a very successful career in journalism. I got so close to finishing my last book, I had even had a great New York Editor, who told me I was going to be "The Voice of a Generation." So much promise I collapse beneath the weight of it. I think they call that self- sabotage.

The last movie my fiancé and I ever saw together was my beloved Nora Ephron's last movie before she died, Julie & Julia, with Meryl Streep and Amy Adams, and he had already called off the wedding we were just spending all this terrible limbo time together, still best friends, and everything was painful, the slow rip apart, knowing everything we did was for the last time, and when we walked out of the theater he was crying, I asked, "What's wrong, besides the obvious?" and he said, "I want you to write your book, I want you to finish things, I want you to accomplish something," and then we were both crying. "I know how much you love Nora," he said, "and how much these movies mean to you, you can do something like this, but... you don't" he said. "And that's what's so hard to watch." There was so much love in his pain.

He knew me, saw me. To lose that is devastating. We were just sobbing in the hot Venice sun, on the sidewalk. And I'm crying again remembering it, remembering Tim and Nora, two forever lost loves. And now I get so close to the men I date, and like a fire I can start but not keep burning, like the book I cannot finish, like something always half baked, half birthed, no follow through. That's what that brass ring symbolized to me and even as we were walking back to his car last night, him laughing saying it was more fun that he'd thought it would be, I think he's always surprised that he likes me, because he can only think about reasons why we don't work- and we are so different, polar opposites, him solar me lunar, yin yang to the extreme. But as we were walking back I couldn't help but think he was thinking about me missing that ring and that paralleled our story, that me and him just never came true—I didn't live up to my promise. And maybe that's because I haven't lived up to so many promises. The ring has slipped through my hands so many times. I'm so afraid of going around and round in life and never getting it. I'm so afraid of always being so close and letting it slip through my hands.

Crumbling Castles and Windswept Bluffs. Herself and her/ They're good together/ they've survived all sorts of weather/ She knows herself/ She knows herself well/ She holds her own hand/ When she goes through hell/ She's knows she's a fan of Scottish landscapes/ Crumbling castles and wind swept bluffs/ People who stand by you/ When the waters get rough.

In saying the hidden words that long to be said/ For we never know how long till we're dead/ In moving the energy to your heart from your head/ And breathing into where it hurts /and getting messy in the dirt/ Great thinkers who happened to be big drinkers/ Who fought the good fight and wrote deep into the night.

People who were cast out/ who found the gift of turning in/The ones who know just how to cross the line/ Rebels with a cause who fearlessly mine/ Their darkness for gold and have vowed to live/ and never get old.

Fire and the sea, when it's blustery / and treasure-chests in shipwrecks/ that's where the gold is, down in the mess/ She loves good ghost stories/ Candlelight, moon light, silks and velvets/ One glass of wine and two hits of a joint/ Lovers that get Straight to the point/ Sultry singer songwriters who dare/ To stare back at you/ Those who don't wince when faced with deep soul/ Because hiding from truth takes such a great a toll.

She loves/ Springsteen and Mitchell/ Witches and bitches - strays and rescues/ the exiled, the underdogs- she means/ the Second-chancers, the phoenixes risen from the dead/ That's her team/ And she's a hard core believer in things that cannot be seen/ And that no dream is more worthy/ than your dream/ She loves Linda Ronstadt- Heart like a Wheel/ And she dies a little when she hides how she feels/ Janis Joplin, Stevie Nicks and Bonnie Raitt/ She doesn't like gossip and she doesn't like hate/ And she believes everyone has a fate/ and with the universe we co-create / And she does believe in a soul mate.

She loves Bob Dylan and The Band- Big Pink/ When she's really quiet she can hear her beloved think/ He's out there, this someone, and she's his moon and he's her sun/ And she loves Neil Young, Woodstock and Topanga Canyon/ The Last Waltz, Joan Baez- Diamonds and Rust/ And she's finally learned that she can no longer trust/ just any one/ It was the sort of lesson she really didn't want to learn/ Indeed it was the sort of lesson that had to really burn. She was a child then/ She's a woman now/ Those were days when she could only cry "Ow"

Most days she feels free/ That's all that matters you see/ Love liberates, fear cages, when she's afraid

Her spirit withers in jail/ but then she remembers / that if you're going to fail/ Fail spectacularly/ Because she usually gets it wrong/ Before she gets it right/That's how she learns// From all those sleepless nights/And while there are times to retreat// There are also times to push back a little / Take up some space/You should never be afraid/ To show your own face.

Avalon /Atlantis and a life forged by fire/ She's been on trial more than once for her desire/ She loves those who aren't afraid of their own dark/ Anais Nin, Mary Oliver, Marion Woodman / Women who serve the great mystery/ And she doesn't say "history"/ She says herstory/ And "Oh my goddess"/ And when she's out of love's alignment/ She makes a big mess/ But She's learned that haters/ Only make you greater/ She believes in skinny dipping under a full moon/ And singing loud even when you're out of tune/ In serious, wise Gold-hearted strong handed men who know how to play/ and when it's hard, how to stay.

That the brave choose joy/ And she will love/ The little boy In him/ And that compassion makes the man/ And while we're here we should forgive all that we can/ That we die in winter and are reborn in spring/ And everyone has A song to sing /And no one can tell anyone/Their song Can't be sung/ And it's not over Until love Has won.]

Fall, Martha's Vineyard, 2012.

Star Seed.

I don't remember much from my childhood or even my early twenties, really I don't, they say that's normal for a Starseed, that gives me comfort anyway, because most of it is just blacked out memory like someone threw tar over the film of my life. But some moments seep through the veil, and I can almost re-enter my body back then, I can remember each of my senses in the experience, they were moments of ceremony, moments where music or ceremony was taking place. Ritual. Ritual called me home to that place I see now in my inner temple, the field in the mist where the beautiful goddesses with long hair and crowns of metal and flowers circle around me, repair me, nurture me, love me and welcome me home. This is my planet. In my childhood I would feel integrated where and when candles were lit, where girls and women wore crowns of flowers in their hair and long dresses and people were singing. In storms and when wind ravaged. I always loved storms, when Mother Nature held court. Times like that my young soul sat up and paid careful attention, felt familiar and a sense of belonging, then "normalcy" took over and I slunk back into my depression, sullenness, and alienation.

But I would re-enter my experience at the ocean or during a certain song, like when Bruce Springsteen sang "The River," as I laid in the way back of the Volvo and my parents drove into the night toward the Island. I remember liking the darkness, the movement, like being back in the womb carried by the mother, with the chilly wind coming through the open windows and being able to see the stars through the glass.

I loved any movie about witches and magic, I devoured Alice Hoffman books when she wrote about women with magical powers living by the sea. I remember feeling like life was a quest, but I didn't know for what or where and how it began, and that I was trapped in the wrong body, life, dimension. I felt I had a role, one I was not yet living. I used to say to my fiancé all the time, "I'm not who I am yet."

When I came out as a witch I asked a college friend if she was surprised and she said, "Not really, you had Practical Magic on endless loop every night."

"I'm something else, there's something else going on inside me, I'm not where I need to be." That's the hum that ran through me for thirty years, the trapped under ice while everyone skated on the pond above me feeling. I remember getting kicked out of a lot of classes early on for not listening, for daydreaming, for challenging the teacher. [I would raise my hand and ask, "how does one person get to tell another person what to do, doesn't what all the other students think, matter too?"] For being so overwhelmed by our viewing of E.T. that I was told to sit outside until I stopped my heaving crying.

For throwing a protest over the science teacher's use of live frogs to dissect, for getting cast out of that room too. Cast out, cast out, cast out, always cast out, the door shut behind me. I sat there slumped against many a door: "You don't belong."

It's how my ancient magical soul began on this earth, cast out of her kingdom, roaming and longing for home and love ever since. Like Lillith cast out of the first garden. The Wild Woman cast out of Patriarchy. The witch hunted for her wild wisdom.

It's how I woke up here, a dark goddess on a quest to heal her wounds and unlock her chains so she could go home. With a vow not to misuse or abuse my powers this time.

I called the earth "down here," starting as a young child - as far back as I can remember, people just kind of flinched when I said it and moved on. This planet always felt like alien territory. I was always asking for a handbook, thinking why isn't there a handbook, feeling like a tourist or a guest. Asking, "how do others know how to live, to be here, and I don't? How come I don't get it? How are they happy living these lives, how are they happy with all the suffering?"

Then that point last year, the ends of the earth, on my knees, "teach me how to live or how to die, I cannot walk any further on this path." And then my awakening. And then thank Goddess for my Ascension. Yes you are an Earth Angel, yes you bear celestial light yes there is an ascension yes you remember eternal things and belong to an eternal home. No this earth is not your "home home" but you will find yourself in her nature, in her green and blue, in your ritual. You have great work to do.

The sky cried all dark and mystical night, there were howling winds sweeping through the torrents of rain and I slept with the windows open to hear her moan and feel her stir the air. Then as day broke there were shots fired at dawn, adding to a night that felt out of Sherlock Holmes on the Moors, but on the bright clear walk to the inlet at nine the streams were bubbling- singing and rushing where yesterday there had been only mud. Things were singing, things were moving, no longer silent and stagnant. Like when we grow from dry and dying to ripe and full of life.

The inlet itself had swelled up the shore over the large rock I usually sit on, it was alive and full with fresh clear water and new life from the rains. The earth knows something about tears, her body full with pools and oceans of salt water, like the kind that runs in our veins. Someone said recently, the greater your capacity to feel the greater your… power. Mama knows how to cry and then use that water to move herself down the river.

When I meditated under that Full Moon in March there came a whisper "Starseed," the first time I ever heard that beautiful term, and then a promise "Welcome Home Goddess, You will find your home soon." Here I am leased to my first home in years that is mine, in the woods by the water in my favorite fishing village in the world. And suddenly tied to one place and grounded, I feel free. With boundaries, I am liberated. Isn't life endlessly beautiful and paradoxical and mysterious, when guided by the strength and love of the Great Mother.

[**Cover Up.** Every one my whole life has said "Cover Up"/ I don't want to see that skin/ I don't want to see that scar/ I don't want to see that pain/ Because when you don't have to see me You don't have to see you/ Everyone Her whole life Has told Her "Cover Up." We don't want to see/ what we fear/ what we desire/ who we are/ what we have done/ what we cannot explain/ what we came from/ and what we will return to [we will kill your chaos and mystery/ with our rules and order] On top of your wet and wild earth we shall build our empires/ we'll suffocate your moist flesh with concrete/ We'll raze your wild dense dark forest/ home of the beautiful the powerful the wild and the free/ down to the ground. And then we'll build our empires on their burial grounds. All hail the boss. We'll shoot your remaining wolves/ from close range/ in helicopters we like to show nature / who's boss/ we like to show the wild,We like to put the wild/ in order. We like to show the feminine/ who's in fucking control here./ We'll send children to war to kill other children. We need to show them / who is boss. All hail the boss/ We'll cover you up/ We'll kill your wild/ When I am talking about/ my power/ I am not talking/ about- and I am not wearing/ a god-damned/ shoulder-padded/ "power suit." No I am not wearing anything/ At all/ I want Love. Not. Power./ The Power. of. Love./ I am talking about my raw internal life giving Shakti. One that needs no clothes to make-up the woman. The make up does not make up the woman.

Not external power/ Internal power/ All my life they told me/ cover up kill your wild/ All my life they told Her/ cover up we'll kill your wild/Cover Up/Cover Up/ Cover Up ["And don't hold me accountable/ for what I might do/ if I see you. I might have to show you/ who's boss."] Cover the scars / the flesh/ the truth/ Cover the wild earth/ and the wild you/Sit down/ Don't speak Up/ Lie down/ Don't stand up/ Well the Feminine, The Indigo, the weird and the wild and the outcast/ have the floor now/ what floor of this planet is left/ For we are its/ last hope/ And it's time for the wild to win/ the voiceless to scream/ the innocents to rise/ the forests to bloom/ the creatures to howl/ and the children to play again. Cover Up, they said/ Well, no. Now it's time to take it all off/ Can you look at me?

Can you look at you?/ Can you look at this world/ It's the only way to save it/ Cover up?

I think not/ Undress from the lies/ stand naked in the truth of you

Would you tell Goddess Kali to go put on a shirt? / She'd sooner make one out of your skin/ And dance on the graves/ of the innocents until they rise/ screaming the victory whoops

of sweet fierce natural justice.]

Martha's Vineyard, Fall, 2012.

Not a Wiccan, But a Witch.

I went to my first Celtic/Pagan/All Female ceremonial gathering two nights ago, it was definitely not a straight up coven honoring Mabon & The Equinox, but they were pagans, earth worshippers, goddesses. I don't fall under one belief either, although often when people hear that I practice ritual and honor with the Mother, they say, "Oh you should meet my friend Becky, she's Wiccan too," without me ever saying I'm "Wiccan," I wouldn't because I'm not.

I'm a witch but I'm not Wiccan. It's kind of like, when people hear I'm single, at 33, they immediately say, "Oh you should meet my one single friend Dave." Or my gay friends who are constantly plagued with "You're a lesbian? My friend Shelly is too, I should set you guys up." Is this just a way of saying, "I don't think you're weird, I know another one like you," or, as also often happens, do people really think that because I practice yoga, I'm going to become best friends with that other woman they know who practices yoga? Does my singledom make them uncomfortable? Of course before I explain that a witch is just a woman aligned with the earth and a natural healer, they shake in their boots from all the patriarchal propaganda they've unknowingly bought into.

But actually people haven't been as weirded out recently, really since the beginning of the year I've seen a LOT of minds expand and people open their hearts a bit more to spirituality. I think when the world is increasingly on fire, more people naturally turn in and ask the big questions. When there isn't anything to lean on externally, they begin to search internally. Which brings me back to this Pagan group - they wore flowers in their hair and their smiles beamed like suns. They were gentle and loving with deep reverence for Nature & Spirit. I called my best friend when I got home and told her all about it, feeling like a high school outcast who was getting closer to finding her tribe, her club, although most of me still resists "joining" things. [Big clue you're a witch, by the way]. It fueled my recent desires to lead my own Moon Nights, meditations and ritual and yoga and circles. My dream is there would be one in towns across the world and we'd all be connected to wish for healing together, Self & Earth, and other high causes, under the New and Full Moons. Soaking in the Moonlight and Raising the Vibration together, powerfully united. This kind of leads me to the whole notion of "coming out" as a witch.

You go through a lot of stages... My whole life I've been drawn... to magic mystery.. witches themselves, but my whole life but was pre-programmed by patriarchal society's lies that witches are bad and ugly. I had no idea what a real Goddess was. For me it started with finally listening to the internal interest a seeking of ritual and belonging, but then an increasing, "Am I? No...I'm making this up. I am just having a minor break with reality." I told myself I was delusional and just needed to believe that I was finding myself and believe in magic because otherwise my world was too dark and heart-breaking, I was so often debilitatingly depressed.

But it persisted, my true self, until I could not call anything a coincidence anymore, until I could not pretend I was pretending anymore. And then I got to a point where I just had to tell people, it was all part of the process of my awakening- but I over did it, as I tend to do, I went on full blast. I wore the t-shirt, got the bull horn out. Went door to door. OK, not really but close. I told everyone, completely out of context with no transition.

My friend who recently gave up alcohol described it like this: "I mean you have to tell everyone, and when you've told everyone in your life you're telling the poor woman at the GROCERY STORE." So I told everyone, "I'm a witch." Most of them were like, duh. But looking back it was all one big soul's homecoming, not necessarily finding

Goddess devotion, but just allowing myself to naturally become what I always was, to follow my intuition through the veils to the Truth.

I don't follow any one book, I mostly practice just what comes through me when I'm out in nature, I stay open and receptive, but often end up on my knees with my hands in the water or the earth, asking for self healing to heal the earth beneath me, my healing is her healing, and tend to the fire inside of me. That's how it went yesterday, anyway, and every day is different. But almost every day I end up in ritual.There's tons of ways to worship the earth and work with spirit, "there are 1,000 ways to kiss the ground, 1,000 ways to go home again," says Rumi.

Nature ritual is how I go home again but it was a pleasure to practice alongside other women. Beautiful, really. I went by myself, brought non alcoholic cider, it was a crisp fall night as I walked up the gravel road that snaked upwards to the house. I heard laughter and children at the top of the hill and I followed the sounds. I'd worn all black with a long cocoon sweater, my hair still drying around my shoulders. The house sat atop the hill, surrounded by trees, it glowed from the inside, a warm orangey light. There were women with crowns of flowers in their hair in long velvet dresses, and one wearing a Stevie Nicks gypsy fringed shawl greeted me. We did an incantation to the

Four Winds almost immediately, like the ones I first did at Kripalu and then in Hawaii with Shakti Sunfire then we took libations of wine and cedar to the trees, the hostess's yard full of tall beauties shooting skyward.

I took cider to two trees wrapped around each other like desperate lovers. I sat at their base as the cider absorbed into the moss and thought about how signing the lease here has made me feel safe, like the world won't be taken from up under my feet again, and how feeling safe heals my root chakra. How without the roots, of course, the plant cannot rise, and I have felt like a rootless tree, a tumble weed in the winds, for far too long. I asked the trees for the depths of their roots and the strength of their spines. I asked for a love like the one I could feel coursing through their veins as they held each other forever.

We made clay animals and read their Celtic totem, we sat molding mother earth in our bare hands as the woman in the gypsy scarf told the ancient fable of Mabon. And even though, as soon as I heard one of the women say we were going to "dance" I made note to slip right on out before that got started, I made myself stay, and instead of terrifyingly awkward it was really beautiful, we all lanced hands and did this sort of trance-like barnyard-esque circle dance together, and I had a 4 year old swinging off my arm like a monkey. For the rest of the night she attached herself like glue around my leg so I had to walk peg-legged, limping like a pirate across the room for food and cider, and to the bathroom and back. Everyone was so nice, the older women especially, but I just played with the little girl, the older women all seemed to know each other, and it was predominantly older women, and the girls who looked about my age all knew each other and talked intimately, so my outsiderness still lingered. After the food- rich warm harvesty food, lots of root vegetables for grounding- I said my thank yous and slipped out, and drove home on the winding tree-canopied roads under a particularly dramatic waxing moon.

Take your salt baths, if you cant swim in the ocean. Salt baths, sage, keeping your rocks and crystals near, all this cleansing, clearing and grounding helps a lot right now. As I first woke up a year and a half ago my intuition was always leading me to salt water for energetic cleansing, I took sometimes three baths a day as I read spiritual books and re-learned how to live. You might feel exhausted, sick, off balance, that's normal. Baths are portals to our rebirth, they soak many old karmas away down the drain, many of you feel drawn to them more than ever now, and Im also cleaning my house- cleaning the internal and external temple as the wheel turns, as we move toward the end of the

Piscean Era, you're truly getting rid of all your old crap, getting scrubbed clean for rebirth and a brand new Act.

Waking up can be an incredibly embarrassing vulnerable time, you start to shout truths that seem so obvious now, but they come through you in such a startling manner, like electricity currents through your system at first. It can feel like being zapped alive like Frankenstein- but you're your own creation- and it's scary but thrilling. It reminds me of Nora Ephron's great line for Billy Crystal in When Harry Met Sally when he rushes to meet her on New Year's Eve, "I came here tonight because when you realize you want to spend the rest of your life with somebody, you want the rest of your life to start as soon as possible." With your newly found self, you're ready to take on the world, you want to Fully Start Living YESTERDAY, to make up for all the time you lost sleeping. You've found a part of yourself you never knew existed, or you wondered, but thought you were dreaming, and you've filled an endless black hole, healed life's persistent empty ache, you've discovered a Lost Secret, and Ancient Door, a Priestess's Tomb inside yourself and you've woken her up and every cell in your being knows This is Only Just the Beginning. It's like romantic love, the whole world shifts the keys to heaven are yours—"So this is what they're talking about"—but you've fallen in love with yourself. All the world is a playground for your dreams, the world isn't just your oyster, you're your oyster. You've woken up, You've saved yourself. It's shout it from the rooftops joy, feeling found. It's Saving Grace, and what is Grace, grace is us what saves us. There is no feeling in the world like saving yourself, like being your own hero. Don't you finally feel ready? "Be not afraid," Joan of Arc would say. "You were born to do this."

[If you get a chance to be brave, take it.

If you get a chance to love, take it.

If you get a chance to grow, take it.]

Martha's Vineyard, Fall, 2012.

Oh the Witches Made Them Feel.

Everyone asks me.

"What's a witch." And sometimes, so often, they laugh nervously. Because they've seen the patriarchal movies and they've dressed as one for Halloween, with green paint and a wart on the end of a long ugly prosthetic nose. And they've called a "bad woman" a "witch."

They have believed, What the patriarchy wanted you to believe. You have been deeply programmed to fear yourself. Even as the judges sentenced them to death, they'd wax poetic about their hair their eyes and the way they made them feel. Oh witches made them Feel

Too Much. Because we fear what we feel. So it was off the to the Gallows with them. A witch is the wild woman.

Who lives in your soul. Full of ancient wisdom, the wisdom of the earth

Awakened at a crucial time when we need to return to the earth

She's the Old Soul everyone has always noticed in you. The one who has been dying to rise and free you for thousands of years. But She had to cover her eyes and sleep eventually

At the horror of what we did to her, of what we have done to this planet, of what we have done to ourselves. For the earth and our bodies are one. And we have brought both to the brink of destruction.

We cannot save the earth without first saving ourselves.

I tried for 30 years to sleep and cover my eyes suppress My Witch. To suppress my Shakti that tried to rise from the base of my spine with sedatives. A lot of women do this. So many of us just want to go back to sleep. But She shook me down till I woke up. She had had enough. She wanted out she wanted to break free to save me. But I was petrified of letting her loose So I drove to the doctor In Beverly Hills for more pills. And I would say, "Its getting worse" and she would say, "so you need more." In other words so you can feel Absolutely Nothing. Because the less you feel

the less powerful you are.

For what would happen when I finally let myself feel is I would break down to wake up.

I would see I wasn't small. I was large. I was the Universe. I wasn't a sheep. I was a wolf. I was the earth. And I had to save her. And I had to save myself.

And this is precisely no this is exactly what they don't want you to know you're not small you come from the stars, and like Hafiz says, you will become one again. If you close your eyes,

you can remember being one

in the endless sky, and you're not a sheep no definitely not-howl growl snarl-You're a wolf.

It's not just that the labels and limits they've given you don't fit- howl growl snarl- it's that

they're just too damn small- for the wild wolf of a woman within you.

Who is not going to give up her fight, until you set her free.

***

[She's a rule breaker and a love maker

and a risk taker and a wisdom waker

and an earth quaker.]

Late Summer, Martha's Vineyard, 2012.

Meeting Kali

I stood at the cove with the wind whipping about so loud it whooshed in my ears and then She licked her flame-tongue at the back of my neck. Cold wind, hot fire, The Dark Goddess is here, riding in on her flames of Just Destruction.

"Are you ashamed?" She asked, a dark, rich, ancient voice, I can feel her cloak billowing behind me, all her dark majesty hovering inches from me and in that I saw a flash, before me, of everything about myself that I had denied and rejected and shamed.

"No," I said, and I turned to greet her. She took me in, we took all the dark into the light and we held it like the loveless abandoned child that it really is, that's all it really is. You're your child. Love You.

[She said, "Please Don't Worry About Me,

That Sends Negative Energy to me You See,

Loved, Whole and Well is How I See you,

And How I Ask for You, to See Me."]

Fall, Martha's Vineyard, 2012.

The Amethyst.

Yesterday I was guided at the Cove to take off my new amethyst, a rich purple chunk of magic, the size of a tiny fist, and offer it to the Dark Goddess beneath the driftwood and shell Priestess Bench. I brought the Goddess a branch of thorns—thorns the mighty protector of the Rose, how dare we love the silky rose and not her thorny protector, the dark goddess protects the light, protects Us. Embracing her, not fearing her, will bring you more power than you thought possible. And then in the late morning light I buried the Amethyst beneath the bench, protecting it by placing it under a horseshoe crab shell and asked it to be bestowed with the power and protection of the Dark Goddess, as night fell I felt weaker without the stone around my neck but was comforted that it slept beneath her spell at the water's edge. This morning there was a message in my heart, "you must grab the stone before noon," so Gracie and I raced to the water, which was warm this morning, and before I uncovered the stone I stripped to nothing and dove in, refreshed, rebirthed.

Naked, I walked out of the water not unlike Viviane, "She Who Lives," the Lady of the Lake, and retrieved the Amethyst, sparkling, blessed, and alive, and returned it to my neck, sitting for a moment with the sun on my wet skin. The day was new, and so was I. After a moment I pulled my clothes back on and on the walk back I stopped, as I always do, before the Triple Goddess tree, a maiden a mother and a crone branching out from the same trunk. "You remember a time when we were worshipped," the tree said, "thank you." The tips of her once green leaves are now bright red, my 33rd Autumn is rushing past as fast as the leaves can turn, blazing brilliantly for a moment and then gone, reminding us so beautifully and bittersweetly, of just how short a time- an unknown amount of seasons left in this great mystery - to make of my life something Magnificent.

[SECRETS OF THE YEWS.

He asked,"Baby, what's the sitch/ with you being a witch" /

I said,"Darling, Let go of your fear

/Don't believe/ Everything you hear/

I'll tell you what it means to me

I'm a nature lover a Goddess worshipper and a tree hugger/

I honor The Mother

Which until now/ In a patriarchal society/

That didn't really fly/ You see?"

I said, "I believe everything has a season/

And there are magical things far beyond Reason

And I don't believe in what you call a coincidence/ I call it synchronicity

And I call on the guidance of the Gods and Goddesses and ancestors/

Who have come before me.

And I bow to all animals and creatures

as our teachers/ from the spider to the fox to the Loon

and I align my life with the phases of the earth and moon.

And then he asked me, "how did you know?"

I said, "well it began to show/

when everyone was lining up/ To hear the father in the pews/

and I was slipping out barefoot/ to hear the secrets of the yews."

Fall, Martha's Vineyard, 2012.

A Channeling

It is all going to be okay and it always will be. There is no problem. There are only solutions. You have everything you need to heal yourself. The answers are in the questions. You are accounted for. We are protecting you, we are huddled behind your purpose, your mission here, we are pulling for and championing your every second of existence. We believe in the love you have to give and the love you are giving. Nothing grows without love and you are planting the seeds. We know the love you have to give has already changed the world, and it is only growing inside of you. By the time you are done here your love will be your legacy. Every time you say "yes" to the unknown (when you are afraid but you know it is right), you are serving your mission. Every time you choose to give instead of take, your heart does a pushup, getting bigger, getting stronger. Every time you choose to love yourself instead of punish yourself, your life force glows and strengthens and calls out, and you raise the vibration.

Keep Going Keep Going Keep Going,

We Love You, Keep Going. For the Planet, *Don't Give Up.*

For the Animals, *Don't Give Up.*

For the Children, *Don't Give Up.*

For Us, *Don't Give Up*.

For You, *Don't Give Up.*

Most people quit

Right before they hit

Gold.

Fall, Martha's Vineyard, 2012.

The Fight for Life.

Two years ago today I got the news that my friend had taken her life. I was in the family cabin in Chilmark, it was a damp dim day like this, I was waiting until the day darkened even more so I could drink wine and let things go fuzzy, not sharp and awful, not terrible and sickly the way they felt and things had felt for years, just holding my breath until I could drink. We had shared a darkness, a fragility, a devastating sadness, hers won that day, finally took her. I had a few days until my first would-be wedding anniversary to the man I thought was the love of my life, I was in the cabin to hide from it as if I could, to drink it away alone. Everything was so bleak, I was sure I had nothing left. No friends, no hope, no life left to live. You know, that final place.

When I woke up today I didn't remember exactly that it was the anniversary of my friend's suicide but my spirit knew. I woke up with Dylan Thomas' poem "Do Not Go Gentle into that Good Night," in my head, they'd read it at my mother's funeral. But today I woke up here alive in Menemsha with Gracie at my feet, I woke up with a fight in my heart. Stand and fight, I heard. Fight. Stand and fight. I knew nothing of the Dark Goddess back then, neither did my friend. I knew nothing of alchemy of pain into gold, of drawing on my destruction for strength, finding the gold in the wreck and of rising from the ashes with more power than ever before. I heard a quote recently, "Survivors are dangerous, for they know they can survive." Well then call me dangerous.

I once chose and was ruled only by fear and I fell down at death's feet when it first whispered for my mother. I never chose to be brave or fight. I never chose light and strength and Love, how I wish I had chosen it for her and our house. When faced with the choice to run or fight I always ran. Tending to anyone sick now I think of my mother alone in bed as her hours ran out, last night in bed after that dark day I felt her pain and her fear to die so young with children and a man she loved and a new career and all I wanted to do was be there for her. But I can't anymore.

When tending yesterday to Gracie all I could do was be haunted by all the ways I could have made things lighter, easier and more comfortable for my mother but instead I denied and I ran. I over-tend to others now, but the one person I really want to love and ease the pain of is gone, that chance to show love came and went. The chance to show love is always coming and going. The regret of not showing love is a deep endless burden, I will do everything I can to not feel that again, the remorse of turning away from need. I will show Love at every turn I am aware of. Be strong, be strong, be strong. It's your turn to stand and fight.

Death is a reminder to get busy loving, loving hard. Nothing has killed you yet. Carlos Castaneda says ""Death is the only wise advisor that we have. Whenever you feel, as you always do, that everything is going wrong and you're about to be annihilated, turn to your death and ask if that is so. Your death will tell you that you're wrong; that nothing really matters outside its touch. Your death will tell you, 'I haven't touched you yet." It hasn't touched me yet, mine or Gracie's or yours. Knowing that it's coming at some point should give me power and courage, not weakness. Knowing death is coming should give me greater life. Two years ago today I was still so raw and deathly I know that could have been me. But now here I am. Miracles happen. You are always coming to save yourself. I am still here with great reason and so are you. I choose love. I choose life. I bow to the earth with gratitude and in the face of all this death and destruction I stand, I stand and fight. I want to crackle with life with every step I have on this earth like Dylan Thomas says I want my words to fork lightning until I am buried, with every breath I have in my lungs. I want to blaze a love trail and start a love fire. Love will be my legacy. I know this light I am in now because I have known dark. Rage against the death, stand in its face. There is nothing enlightened about shrinking,

Marianne reminds us. We don't all get to make it to the other side, I did. I was saved. Now what will I do with my second chance. How dare I ask for anything more than these riches I have now. I am walking gratitude today, I am walking faith. I'll be your angel, I'll be my angel. I feel the Dark Goddess hiss at death, unafraid, I hear her fire crackle. I have not come this far to back down now. I will never go gently into the dark again. I'll fight for you, I'll fight for my mother, I'll fight for my unknown love and my unborn children and I'll fight for this earth and all its innocents. I'll fight for Gracie and I'll fight for Jessica. I'll fight for myself and in that fight I know I fight for all of us. Darkness cannot hide that truth any longer, that my battle for self is my battle for us all.

[She said one day your pain will heal the world. One day your wounds will turn to gold. That is your alchemy. You turn fear into love. You channel the messages, from above. You lived it so you could learn it so you could teach it. One day the wounds you touch will turn to gold.]

Winter 2012. Amrit Yoga Institute, Florida.

Learning by Love.

Teach love, not fear. My best teachers have always loved me unconditionally, seen the higher parts of me and opened me those undiscovered parts of myself. My worst teachers have lorded over me with fear, and I closed up tight, sheltered myself against them and their teachings. I might have momentarily obeyed to get out unscathed, but I never Learned, because I wasn't open, I was closed, contracted in fear. Not open, the way love opens you. Fear never taught me anything but more fear/resentment. Like my teacher says, "I am not here to teach you, I am here to love you. My love will teach you." Love is the greatest healer and the Greatest Teacher. I am blessed to have found a teacher who loves me without condition and leads me back home to me, who keeps the doors of his heart open to me at all times- not one who demands I follow his rules to support his ego. And the greatest teachers, they want you to leave them. To evolve and share your teachings.

I am remembering one professor in college who held me back after class to scream at me. "You'll never be a writer," he fumed, red in the face, spitting. "How dare you even call yourself one?! You don't follow any rules! Who the hell do you think you are, you can't even form a proper sentence!!!" I cried for days and the wound didn't heal for ten more years, every time I thought of it I shuddered from the trauma. It certainly didn't encourage me to write. I was a lost depressed Indigo child flailing in the patriarchal college system, and he was a strict angry member of a crumbling system who couldn't have resented me more. His hate did not teach me anything but fear. So I am so blessed to have found my Beloved Teacher who has shown me self love through his love. Because he sees God in all, he sees the light in me. He reflects my higher self back to me, he sees all the Divine parts I wasn't sure were there - I had caught glimpses of them and I had only hoped they existed. He has pulled them out of me and made them real. Fear builds walls, love breaks them down. Teach with love.

[When you're at the end of your rope/ For Goodness sakes/ Let go.]

Winter, 2012, Martha's Vineyard

Always Been Different.

I remember starting to realize I was different from other kids my age once on the school bus in third grade. I was sitting next to a well-adjusted little blond girl with straight smooth hair, soft tan skin and sleek brown eyes. I was a sad dreamy little

Indigo child, not that we knew that then. It sure would have helped, maybe saved me years of attempting to "normalize," with pills and frat boys and psychiatrists and corporate jobs. I was staring at the green trees whizzing past outside the window while playing curiously with a cut inside my mouth with my tongue. It was a fresh wound, it stung each time I touched it. I remember turning to the girl on the green plastic bench next to me, her name was Kelly, and asking,

"Do you ever play with things even though it hurts?" I asked, running my tongue once more along the cut.

She stiffened, "No," she said, looking at me like a freak, "Never."

I knew I had taken a chance, she seemed like the kind of girl who could avoid looking at her pain her whole life, and be fine, just like that, never wanting to know what was on the other side, what lurked in the shadows. Even back then I knew that would never be me, something about me loved the darkness, explored the depths of the Underworld. I sunk back toward the window feeling wrong, bad, weird.

[I CAN'T LOSE ME FOR YOU. No baby it's you / Who doesn't understand/ I don't have time / to die for a man/ and you cant break a heart thats already been blasted/ wide fucking open / and I can see and feel everything from here/ and it all just so crystal goddamn clear/ That there is nothing left to fear/ And that I can stand to lose you / But can't stand one more time/ to lose myself/ for a man.]

Martha's Vineyard, Winter, 2012.

Everything Always Comes Full Circle.

At the water this morning the air was cold, so I shut the car door after I let Gracie out, hoping she might just run around while I finished my coffee. Instead, she walked up to my window with a look of panic in her eyes. And that's how she told me, 'this is how it happened,' how she was abandoned in Nebraska, how she ended up a street dog. As I speak less, I hear so much more. The less I say, the more I feel. Less is so much more.

She was driven somewhere, and left. It explains her abandonment issues, and also her fear of driving. But if she'd never been left on the side of the road somewhere, she'd never have been in that Omaha pound, and I'd never have crossed her kennel two weeks after I got there, uprooted, knowing no one except my touring boyfriend, needing a companion.

Someone let her go so she could come to me, even if they didn't know what they were doing. Now she roams the beaches of Chilmark, sleeps beneath the covers, is loved, fed, kissed in excess. She has, as they say, "arrived." It came full circle this morning, to finally, finally forgive those who have "abandoned" us, for they were on their paths, doing what they felt called to do for their soul, and as they liberated themselves they were liberating us into a new story, a higher story, a greater story.

That person who "ended" it, who let you go, was beginning a new story for you, even if they acted unconsciously, they too were being guided. We cannot hold onto the side of the riverbed forever, that will tear us apart. We have to let go and be taken with the river. I thank the person who abandoned Gracie, not knowing they were gifting her to me, us to each other. I thank that one time boyfriend, then fiancé, for his abandonment of me. I thank him for starting me on my journey toward Self, Wholeness, All-oneness. Thank you for leaving me so I could find myself.

It was so terrifying to head straight into darkness to discover myself, I might have put it off forever if I could have. He let me go so I could get here- down through my underworld, back up to the surface. This was a solo journey, it had to be, we could not carry each other to where we each had to go. Without forgiveness, seeing their innocence, seeing yours, you are tethered to the ground, stuck, sickened, looking backwards. Who do you still speak of with anger, blame, or harden your heart to?

On a more physical note, my body is changing again, rounding out into a fullness I've been resisting because of yes, society's messages that I should be thin to be beautiful.

That women should be small and take up very little space. Eff that. Be big. Take up space. Heading home from the water I looked at a sign I always pass, this time differently. "Beware of Curves," it said. And I smiled, imagining the ancient symbol of the Goddess, that divine woman symbol all boobs and hips, curves and swagger. Yes indeed, I thought, beware of all that curvaceous, feminine, divine power, for it's most certainly here. Be Full. Fill yourself up of life, your dreams, and love. Be full so you can be of service. Receive so you can give.

[PART ONE. COMFORTABLE. My whole life they've told me / play nice smile act normal/ lighten up stay in the shallow end and on the shore stay only in the light and on the surface/ do what the others do wear a bra/ and would it kill you to brush your hair. because it will make us comfortable. but I am not here to make you comfortable/ I am here to wake myself up / and it's not Comfortable/ no not at all/ and if my roaring rousing waking/ wakes you up/ in the process / Well I guess that's good/ Even if it's gory/ For birth is both gory/ and glorious/ no love no glory/ no gory no love/ for love is both gory/ and glorious/ They said you're too edgy but I said why/ isn't the edge where you finally learn to fly/ I am not The sort of woman/ You come Around/ If you don't Want to change/ Perhaps That's/ Why So Few Do/ I/ will not go To you/ You have To come To me/ I am not The sort of woman/ You want to be around If you don't want/ To question Yourself Because I am Always/ Questioning/ Everything About Everything Including especially/ myself/ And all my life they said "Clean Yourself Up"/ But I just rolled in the dirt I just got closer to God/dess/ And they said "cover up and be quiet"/ in the face of all my flesh and all my feeling/ Well I just Took my clothes off/ And I just cried out / And I just/ got even closer/ To God/dess/ "Be a lady"/ but I just protected myself and I just provided/ for myself/ it was masculine/ and it felt whole it felt

Divine/ change isn't comfortable/ but I know I have to keep changing myself/ to change the world/ because I'm not comfortable/ with how the world is/ and I don't understand/ how anyone else/ can be either.]

Martha's Vineyard, Later Winter, 2013.

Clean Living, Clean Service.

I'm back to clean living and clean service, and I never want to NOT be bone- weary again, for all I want, all any one deeply desires, is to be of use, of service, of purpose. So I'm headed to bed soon but the other day I forgot to tell you- you are the only one who can make a difference, a profound, crucial, ripple-effect difference.

The lesson came twice in one day, as the synchronicities do when you are awake in your heart and living from there. I drove down Island to the grocery store, and passed an elderly man on the side of the road with his brown paper bag, he hitch hikes a few times a week down to the store. I passed him and tried to avert his eyes, you know how we do, Normally- "I would but I have a dog in the car, I have stuff in the passenger seat, I'm in a hurry." But he looked me right in the eye and I knew what I was meant to do, of course, we always do, and when we don't do it, that regret doesn't leave us. So I passed him, and I ran one errand but I told myself I'd pick him up on my way back if no one else had. "If no one else does," I said. And lo and behold, on the way back, there he stood, hand outstretched, and no one else had. And so I slowed, and I opened the door for him, and man was he grateful, and also, of course, a Buddhist, and I learned from him.

That evening I took Gracie for a walk and saw a piece of plastic in the dirt road, and I always always always pick up litter but that night I decided to test the world as well, "I'll wait one night and see if anyone else picks it up," I thought. But of course, first thing in the morning, on our walk, there it was. No one else picked it up, it just sat there, polluting the Mother, the toxic plastic digging into her flesh. So I grabbed it and I knew to tell you the unmistakable lesson that no one no one no one else is going to pick it up but you. No one else is going to help but you. You're the hope. You're your, you're this world's last chance. You see it because you are meant to see it and it is yours to heal and it is yours to help and you are the only one who will.

You make all the difference in the world. Pick it up. Reach out. Open the door. Lean in, Engage, Don't even look around to see if anyone is watching or if anyone else can do it or if anyone else is coming. Without pause, dive in and help. This is our last chance, your last chance, the only chance. You are the only hope this world has. Make no mistake, no one else is coming to save it but you. If we don't heal it today, there is no tomorrow.

[Everything falls apart/ When you forget who you are/ Then everything comes back together /When you Remember.]

Martha's Vineyard, Winter, 2013

Sedating Shakti.

My addiction to pills was always sedatives. Xanax, Klonopin, Valium. I didn't know I was always trying to sedate this gigantic spirit inside of me. I think so many women try to sedate their true wild unknown selves. I knew what was in me was big, unfamiliar, wild, and voracious. I was frightened of her, it, me. She wanted so much from me, she wanted so much of life. So I sedated my Self as much as possible, and some days, many days, wished to just go to sleep forever. I used to think to myself, "You can't let women like me sleep, you can't let us sleep." And now I know why. The world needs our Shakti, that shuddering life love force, to bring the planet back to love and life. Thank Goodness I didn't go to sleep forever. Thank Goddess I woke up.

["What happened to you?" He asked. "What do you mean?" She said. He said, "well you're so different my dear/ I can feel your galactic heart from here/ And your skin it glows like the moon/And your eyes, they're enchanted like the sea." /"Oh that," she laughed, "Is because I found the Goddess within me."]

Martha's Vineyard, Winter, 2013.

Remembering Scotland.

I have really been called to look at my past lives recently, and see what my repeated "stories" were, what wounds and samscaras I have awoken in this lifetime to heal, what patterns I am here to break my spirit free from. I feel like I am here for nothing less than full-soul liberation, and to help heal the masses. Tonight in my hot bath the veil felt thinner than ever, I was seeing a vision being a witch in Scotland a long long time ago, I was in a hot bath in a dark bathroom, my hair was long and black, there were golden flickering candles everywhere. Mid-meditation I put my finger on my heart chakra, and I heard, "If you wanted, you could remember everything." I think that's true. I think we already know what wounds we are here to heal. Ask in, it's right there. True liberation lies behind your fear. Fear is the Gatekeeper. Walk through. If the message has been anything, it's been, Don't Be Afraid to Remember, and Don't Be Afraid to Change. Everyone deeply knows their core wound. Everyone deeply knows, who they are.

[Are you a good mother to yourself? Do you rest when you're tired and nourish yourself well? Do you listen to yourself, your sorrows and your dreams, and tuck yourself in sweetly at night? Do you console yourself? Protect yourself? Do you take loving mothering care of yourself? Only when you are good mother to yourself can you be a good mother to the world.]

Late Winter, Martha's Vineyard, 2013.

It's All Between You and the Angels

When I started to wake up two springs ago I suddenly knew it all was only between me and the angels, the way I lived my life. I had a host of them watching, I could feel them on my back, in the sky, hovering, angels and God and Goddessses, watching my every move. It started in that small pottery studio I woke up in. They hovered in the rafters. Every step I took, every action, every word, witnessed. There was nothing that wasn't seen, there was nothing un-watched, un seen, no thought missed or overlooked, nothing. As soon as you realize they are there, You realize there is no more and there never was any, "getting away with anything." Every act becomes holy. It is between you and God, the Goddess, and the angels, how you live. You see an ant flailing to live, you pick it up and move it outside, a butterfly in a puddle, you move it to safety until its wings dry. You see an old woman reaching for juice at the store, you reach for it for her. You see a way you can help, and you do. You never ever want the feeling again of "I could have helped, but I didn't." You feel them watching your life on earth, and you know that's where your contract lies, between you and them, not you and the passing thoughts of others. It is most certainly not about how or what others think of you, but between you, your highest self, God and the angels.

[The Dying Room. She looked around the dark living room / where they sat passed out in the TV glare/ with buckets of factory farmed chicken bones for dinner fare/ littered at their feet empty bottles of soda scattered on the couch /and the television yelling full blare/ an infomercial with a woman in heavy make up to cover her up and heels so high they made sure to cut her off from the earth /she was selling plastic hoarder ware/ to fill the landfills as the A/C pumped Ice Cold manufactured air/ into their lungs while it shot CO2 out into the soft twinkling night/ where the flowers beneath the window gave up their fight/ and gave into their toxic death/ And she said to no one in particular, for no one was listening or taking a breath, "is this a living room or this a dying room."]

Martha's Vineyard, Spring, 2013.

Looking in the Magic Mirror.

This morning I walked into the bakery behind a sleepy woman with wild brown hair, and I felt a pull like the tide toward her energy. She was wearing silky clothes she'd slept in and she walked like she was still dreaming, softly, slowly. She wore loose flowing goddess pants and a soft worn blouse that fell off her shoulders, no bra, her wild knotted hair falling onto her back. She was unapologetically all primal woman, I realized. She carried a beaten wallet and an old coffee cup, she shuffled in front of me for her refill, she said hello again to the girl at the counter. When we walked out it was side by side and as we stepped off the porch she smiled at me with recognition, and as she looked at me, her smiled widened until it was a full to the brim knowing grin. She was me. I was her. So familiar, such a reflection. We were home in silence together for a second.

And yesterday I ran in there for coffee and I walked in behind a woman so blond and pale she glowed like some sort of moon creature. I couldn't see her face but she commanded an energy attention, and she too pulled me into her orbit as I slowed down behind her. Leaving, I saw why. She walked out right in front of me and held the door, absently, for me. But I saw her familiar, small slightly freckled, manicured hand on the doorknob, that was the first breath I lost, then I saw the loosely knitted soft white sweater that hung from her sweet small frame, then the hair, soft white blond, pulled back from her pale face, and the face- the thin painted red lips, the small delicate, perfect little nose, the wide blue eyes—she was the spitting image of my mother. I looked at her wide-eyed, incredulous, she smiled sweetly like you would at a lost dog, then stepped off the porch. I lost my breath completely and staggered to my car where I cried until I could drive. My eyes burned, my heart burned, to feel as if I had seen her alive once more, walking the earth. Still living, getting coffee, headed to the water, on her favorite island, smiling, home. I even had that moment, of, could she still be here and my God, what would that be like? Everything, everything, would be different. That is how much you matter to those who love you. Your leaving leaves a hole in their world. Your leaving shatters their heart into pieces they will spend the rest of their lives putting back together. and the cracks will always show. Their love for you is That. Big. Never forget that, they hold you. You hold them. Touch them gently, and carry them with care.

Martha's Vineyard, Spring, 2013.

Watching Dad Dance.

I've seen my dad dance once, in the light of a barn, at a wedding, just two minutes of moving to music, self-consciously, half his body asking to let go, the other sternly telling it no. I've seen him at the edge of the water, just him and the great unknown, then watched him back away. And I've thought about why I live at the water and it's the only place I feel I can, how baked in and trapped I feel anywhere else, and I live here because it is the literal edge, the physical edge of the world. And the literal deep. And I like walking the edge and I like it where it's deep. The unconscious, the wild depths, what rises from up beneath, what sees all from below. All that treasure in all those shipwrecks. The gold is in the wreck, in our wrecks is where we find our gold. Where Virginia finally drowned all her sorrows, where mother lost her wedding ring and spent all night searching the bottomless wet sand, because she knew what a sign was and she wanted to fight the fates, where men and women have disappeared forever, called out there into the unknown, where people have wished and hoped for each other and promised themselves to change. Being so close to great mystery and great danger and unlimited potential. It's as close to a frontier as I can feel. But I'm always still pushing for more, feeling like there is so much more, I've been there, I'll be back. And it's like Dad has to stay on shore, with a daughter like me, because someone needs to throw the life raft out when I get in over my head, or caught in a rip, or go too deep and can't swim back. And it seems to happen often, and just when I think he can't hear me anymore, I'm too far gone, I've really done it this time, he tosses me a jacket or a rope and brings me back where it's safe. There is the shore, and there is the depth, and just like everything else in this life, you can't have one without the other.

[**A Note.** I had a dream where you crossed a dark and crowded room to me/ in that bar down by the water/ to where I stood alone/ in the back in the corner. And you took a note out of your pocket and handed it to me/ and you looked me alive in the eye / and then you turned and left without a word/ And then alone in my car/ under the cold night sky, my breath in the air, I unfolded the paper and read/ *"I know who you are"* you said/

"So you no longer have to feel dead"/

and I cried warm tears/ that thawed my frozen face/ and brought me back to life/ for I had been seen/ and was no longer/ shivering in solitude.]

Martha's Vineyard, Summer, 2013

We Don't Have to Cower in Fear Anymore.

I don't have to try to too hard to remember the past life pain, for modern witch hunts happen all the time. We all come from the same wound. Let's allow each other to come home to our places of power, to return to our thrones. Let's let each other back in, let's help each other heal & rise.

Her rising is Your rising.

Dear you who have been burned, I was too. We don't have to cower in fear or point the finger anymore. We don't have to hysterically rally each other against each other anymore. We don't have to drive the strong & sexy & earth & different & wise & beautiful & independent & strange out anymore. We don't have to send them away because we can't look in the mirror at what we could be if we were free.

At the raw delicious creative sensual sexual wild mirror of true femininity - anymore.

We don't have to be afraid of our own power anymore. Let's look at each other in awe and not in fear. Who told you to fear each other to compete with each other that a powerful woman was a bad woman.

We don't have to see one woman's raging light and call it the devil. We can end witch hunts right now- only women can stop the witch hunts. We don't have to witch hunt because we were once witch hunted, for our voices that spoke truth, for our beauty as powerful as the sea, our wisdom as wise as the earth, for our strength to birth life, and our magic to change the world.

I don't have to see you as a threat anymore. Your largeness only makes me reach higher your brightness only lights my path further. I choose to see you as an example of pure possibility, as a light, as the feminine unbridled, as a hope, as a symbol of our power, healing, sisterhood and evolution. Thank you for your light- for your big beautiful life- that has pierced the dark sky of patriarchy and shown the way out. I'm not jealous.

I'm inspired.

Let's inspire each other with our fire,

and Not Put the fire under each other.

Dear you who have been burned, I was too. Let's heal and no longer

hurt each other. Because we share the same wound, we were burnt at the same stake.

I love your fire. Burn bright sister. Your flame lifts me higher.

[**PART II. LIKE A WOLF.** When you reach that place of hunger / beyond what any food sex pills or wine can fill- and believe you me I've tried you're at a soul- level hunger and you're hunting down the dream that haunts you the dream you were born to birth that will quench / that will fill this delirious and certain ravenous hunger- I am hungry like a wolf for a dream I have seen Inside of me all I have is my dream /and believe you me my dream has me pinned to the ground to birth it. I am hungry for a world for the world that is growing inside of me In am birthing the woman/ I was born to become/ She is all silk and magic/ she is all waves and freedom/ I am hungry like a wolf/ for the man of my dreams/ The male me/ I met under the moon/ I can feel his presence/ Like a spirit/ Hovering, he's coming soon/ If my life were a house/ It would be haunted with him/ His ghost always just in the next room/ I just heard his footsteps in the hallway /And some days I am patient as a priest for him/ Other days I am foaming at the mouth like Kali for him/ But when I have fully arrived/ So will he / For that's how these things work/ at least for me/ You have to know who you are/ to know what you want/ so you can't get what you want/ unless you know who you are/ And I've seen who I am/ and she no longer just rises momentarily like a mythical creature from the bottom of the sea/ {"did anyone else / see that / but me?}/ no she stays now/ for days and days/ and I've seen what I want/ and I can smell the air/ of the world in which I'll be/ and I am hungry/ like a wolf/ for this world inside of me/ that was once only visible-in/ but is now becoming/ day / by day/ visible out.]

[She said, "when one soul wakes it shakes another. If we can change our lives we can change the world. My change is the world's change."]

Martha's Vineyard, Fall, 2013.

Fuck It. Be Fearless.

I think the best thing that happened to me at Kripalu two years ago was when I was sitting in a Dani Shapiro writing workshop, and we were talking about the task of writing about what mattered to us the most- essentially those parts of us and stories from our lives we were most afraid of. The times that had changed us. A lot of women had questions how to do this - they didn't feel strong, brave, or worthy enough to face their darkness. "How do I face the worst parts of me?" they asked. "How do I write through it?" "How do I mine the darkest days of my life for the gold?" Then a brave pale beautiful woman who had recently survived a brain aneurysm raised her hand behind me. Even as her voice shook, she offered, "what about, just, 'Fuck it. Be fearless?"

Dani was quiet, and then she nodded. "Yes," she said. "Write that down in big huge bold letters and tack it over your desk: "Fuck it, be fearless.'"

[**HE CAN KEEP HIS COOL.** He walked away so cooly/ like none of it ever happened/ He barely looked back- although he did- just for a second, but he winced, like I blinded him. And then he moved on. So.Cool./ And the Goddess said, "He can keep his cool and you you can keep your fire."/ He said I was "too much," it made me wonder if his heart was too small/ He said I was "too deep" /it made me wonder if he was too shallow / and never got went all the way in/ Which is the only way -all the way- for me so / I knew/ He could keep his cool /and I would keep my fire.]

Martha's Vineyard, Fall, 2013.

Bleeding Paws.

I haven't gotten a manicure since my awakening. I can't even stand the smell of nail polish or imagine the feeling of the chemicals on my nails. I have preferred bare nails, bare feet, bare skin, wild hair, a wild, distinctly unmanicured life. But yesterday I gave Gracie a manicure, a toe nail trim, and I was careless with one of her nails, I was in the middle of moving and I was a sweaty hasty mess. She proceeded to bleed profusely, all over the floor of where we were moving out, and her eyes seemed to say, look at all this waste this haste is making. And while I stopped it for a bit with baking soda and a makeshift wrap, as soon as we made the trip up island she started to bleed all over the floor of the new cottage as well. Nothing helped but the landlord's little girl- innocence and the divine feminine herself, a barefoot sprite with a heart so huge you can hear it thumping through her chest- who played doggie nurse while I unpacked, but as soon as she went home to bed the bleeding picked up again. In the morning, we did what we should have done much earlier, we headed to the point where the salt water licked and healed her wound and the sand matted over it as natural dressing, I watched as Mother Nature did what she did best, healing and taking care of her own, far faster and more effective than anything found on the internet. This is a self healing Universe, a teacher of mine says, if you let it be. Stay out of Nature's Way.

There is a common theme in my dreams of late, which are more potent and clear than ever. The last two nights I've lead a group of women into a house, like a large sprawling court room, and once in the house an angry mob turns on me. A man, a lot like that college professor who once grabbed me by the collar and screamed, red-faced, "You'll never be a writer, you can't even form a proper sentence." The leader of the mob booms over the crowd at me, "How dare you disgrace the house of patriarchy, how dare you break our rules," and an angry mob descends upon me. But last night in the dream they didn't succeed in chasing me out, the walls of the house started breaking down, crumbling, and then suddenly we were all standing in the wild free open air, where I was safer, we were safer, stronger, more protected, than we'd ever been in the patriarchal house, and we stood our ground on and for Mother Earth.

[Deep See Diving. Last night I had a dream I was deep sea diving, or deep see diving, going down into the very depths of the ocean to its bed and bringing up life, handfuls of rich nutrient drenched food, for all of us, for consciousness, for the new earth. I would rise to the surface , offer it, take a deep breath, then plunge back down.]

Fall, Martha's Vineyard, 2013.

Power is Inside

When I got back from west coast, from the disaster that was my would-be wedding, to find myself in a Brooklyn basement apartment under a bridge, its concrete sidewalks littered with trash, the building lorded over by a racist drunk homophobic misogynistic landlord. I had no identity except "his ex," and no job and no child and no anything I was supposed to have at the age of thirty in this culture, I felt like a total failure. And I died, I died on that floor. I failed at dreams that had never even been mine.

How was I ever supposed to realize them, if I didn't truly deep down believe in or want them? I was only following the rules handed to me by the iron fist of Patriarchal culture. And I did not domesticate well. I felt suffocated in houses with white picket fences and by jobs with white male bosses and other women who hated me and were threatened by my untamable nature. I wasn't ever going to fit in the domestic patriarchal world- I was wild. I was a wildfire. So I tried my hardest to tame myself. I still had white pills pumping through my blood to sedate the Shakti inside me, the screaming Kali, the loving fierce Durga, the sensual Aphrodite, the endless archetypes of Goddess within me.

I had been magic until about seven years old, and then I opened my eyes and looked around- this was not a world that I belonged to or remembered, I truly remembered the wild mystical land of the Goddess. I didn't belong in the concrete wasteland of father patriarchy I belonged in the wild arms of mother nature. By the time I was eighteen I began to "party" (that always struck me as oxymoronic, shouldn't a party be joyous?) through my life, and my career as a rock journalist enabled that. I sedated myself and drank through it, Marilyn and Stevie Nicks style but not nearly as glamorous, it was my attempt at creating an alternative universe, not knowing yet there was an internal alternate one, not yet knowing how to find that.

But there is no stopping the waking. When my inauthentic life fell apart, I was terrified- where would a woman like me fit? I would have to strike off and create an entirely different, new place for myself.

The witch whispered to me. They had buried the witch so deep down in the tomb of this culture. They had propagandized Her enough to stigmatize her as ugly and evil, so we might stay far away from her self-empowering magic. A little digging into my own soul and history- or herstory books- proved different. She was a beautiful woman, a mirror of the earth who worked with nature- she was autonomous unto her self. She did not bow to patriarchal culture, its limitations and conformity, which is why she had to be killed.

So, who was the witch? I was startled to find- I was the witch. And it was the first and only thing that ever made sense in my life. What was I going to do with this information? The wisdom of the earth, the wisdom of the ancients, sacred powerful information. I was the keeper of something ancient tribal and magickal it would be my work to open the tomb, Pandora's box of feminine magick, unleash it first in my heart and then in the hearts of any women who felt called to hear my song.

My bibles became Women who Run with the Wolves and Dancing in the Flames. My teachers became Marys– Mary Magdalene and Marion (a name which means, "star of the Sea") Woodman, nature's scribe Mary Oliver and Marianne Williamson- any "MA"s who taught of the ways of the Mother. And my true teacher of nature, the wild heart of the feminine, became Martha's Vineyard in Massachusetts. And the spirit of Martha, on that island, was no lightweight.

Patriarchal power is external – the power is outside oneself, it's placed in money and materials and the Man. I woke to the power of love, found it internally, and became, like the witch, autonomous. It is matriarchal in nature to become self empowered.

When our power is external, outside ourselves, we are limited. When our power comes from within, then we are limitless.

Finally, I took it all off. The make up, the heels, the false dreams, the lies, the veils between truth and the veils between me and other and the Mother. We owe such destruction of egoic veils to Goddess Kali, and she continues to whittle me down to my truth. I was naked. I died to the lies to become my truth. And I was held in Her womb on a magical feminine island where I was reborn as my true self- wild, and one with the Mother.

[She said the Answer doesn't have to be mysterious or strange. Your life will change when you change.]

Martha's Vineyard, Fall, 2013.

Open up When Pain Knocks.

Pain, however it manifests, depression, anxiety, longing, fear, worry, is a messenger. Just like that UPS guy/gal on your porch. They have a job to do and it's to Deliver. You gotta look at the package - "oh yeah, that's for me"-

and sign for it and take it in so he can report back and say it's done it's job. The only way to get the pain off the porch is to receive it like the messenger it is.

"Why are you here?"

"How can I help you, what's the message, so you can go home?"

Otherwise, it's gonna hover on your porch and just knock louder

and louder and louder.

Open up to the knocking/nagging and receive the message. It's just doing its job. Only then can it leave you in peace. Pain is just holding wisdom for you to receive.

If it triggers or terrifies you open your heart and stare at it.

When the pain comes, don't close the door

Open up, ask it what its there for

Then sprawl out on the floor

and let the wisdom seep into every pore.

Martha's Vineyard, Spring, 2014.

I'm Not Perfect, Still I Rise. Jai Maya.

I'm not perfect. I've sought love outside of myself as if it could save me. Only my love can save me. I'm not perfect. I've sought external approval despite it coming and going like the tide. I've sought out instead of in. I'm not perfect. I've numbed myself with substance and food time and time again when I was terrified of what I felt. But that doesn't fill the love-hole inside of me, only I can fill that, only God can fill that, and food and substance doesn't protect me from life, nothing can. I don't want to be. I'm not perfect. I've gotten wasted to run from the monsters but they only get bigger and they only get faster. And every time, I said it was "the last time." But while I'm here, I want to open my heart and say "yes," and "thank you," and I want to be naked with the universe. I'm not perfect. I've gossiped, which is witch-hunting other women. And then I only hurt myself. They are me and I am them. When I hurt you I hurt me. So often we fear the mirror. I'm not perfect. I wrestle with a spiritual ego. Thankfully Kali kills is, it is so painful and isolating. I don't want to be on a shaky pedestal, I prefer the earth. I'm not perfect. I once didn't understand there was no difference between a secret and a lie. Kali also showed me that. I learned that lesson so deep it branded me for life. I'm not perfect. I once had frenemies, friends with agenda, friends out of ego or fear. Now if you're in my life I only want the highest for you. I'm not perfect. I can channel the divine but I'm so fucking human. I'm not perfect. I'm a medicine woman who sometimes forgets to take her own medicine. This makes me sick. Then when I take my own medicine, I heal. I'm not perfect. I can give but have trouble receiving. I'm not perfect. I've said what I thought others wanted to hear and not what I truly felt. I went for the correct answer instead of the truth. But that was only speaking the language of fear, a teacher taught me that. I'm not perfect. I've doubted myself and my path and love time and time again. The lesson won't leave until you've learned it. Nothing changes until you accept it. I'm not perfect. When things are going too well I self-sabotage and want to run. I'm not perfect. There are days that I don't get out of bed but tell others to rise. I'm not perfect. I have reached into the known of my past when I was too scared to live in the unknown of the present. That hurt like hell. I'm not perfect. I've wished for normalcy when I was too scared and tired of being different. You don't fit in because you are spectacular. Spectacular, but not perfect. I've fought hard for equality then laid down for men who didn't fight for it themselves. That also hurt like hell. No more sleeping with soul strangers. I'm not perfect. I'm not perfect at all. I've sought the love of people who didn't love me and ignored the love of those who did. I'm not perfect. Sometimes I push others to speak their truth while I cower in the corner in fear. I've let what others think about me matter more than what I know to be true. I'm not perfect. I've placed my worth on my external looks and others' worth on their looks as well. But the heart is all that matters. The soul. I know this, but I forget. Because I'm not perfect. I am terrible at confrontation, I shake and shrink and close my eyes and wish I could fall through a trap door. I'm not perfect. I have Money issues and Men issues and Mother issues. The three M's. But I'm working on them. I'm not perfect. I tell you to speak your voice but even as I write this, I wonder who the fuck am I to write this, and I think of others saying "who the fuck does she think she is." And they do, and they do, all the time. But still I rise. I'm not perfect. But still I write. Still I speak. I am you and you are me. My story is your story. And it's not perfect. But it's sacred. You have a right to tell your story and no one can tell you you're telling it wrong.

I'm not perfect.

But I'm still a phenomenal woman.

I'm not perfect.

But my voice still counts and my voice still matters.

I'm not perfect.

But still

I rise.

Always.

Thank you Maya Angelou, Always & Forever.

Your words changed my life.

I'm not perfect, but still, for you and for me and for us for She,

I rise.

Jai Maya. What if you hadn't raised your voice you would not have raised our souls.

Now for you, I raise my perfectly imperfect voice.

The world needs yours.

Jai Maya.

[She said, Darling, Darling, Everything has a season, and Darling, Darling, Everything has a reason. I wish for you to be loved/ Just as You Are/ And not how you might or could be/ I pray for you for a Love as deep as Strong and Healing as the Sea.]

Martha's Vineyard, Winter 2014.

The Heart of the Feminine.

She stumbled in, clutching her chest, gasping for air, and fell on her knees at the Witch's feet.

"Can't you help me, please help me, please take out my heart, please give me a new one."

The Witch looked down, serenely, knowingly, but not moving a muscle. "Tell me, What is wrong with the one you have?"

"It hurts, I'm in pain, it feels too much."

"Ah, the heart of the Feminine " said the woman in velvet, on her throne, with hair that fell to the floor where the animals slept in her shadow. "Precisely what the world has been waiting for."

The young woman looked up through a veil of tears. "It's not broken?"

"Why yes, but broken open. And now it's working perfectly. The more it feels, the better it works. The more it opens, the greater the power. We need more hearts like yours in the world, and certainly not less. Now carry your blessing back out into the world, let time do its healing, it will turn your sorrow to wisdom, your pain to gold, and where your tears fall, life and love will bloom."

[**SOUL STRANGERS.** The morning light was falling over the unmade bed/ He raised his large marbled arm off my hip/ to rub his eyes open "What's on tap today?" He asked, which was how he began most morning conversations. I made light of myself/ to keep him in the dark/ I played small

so he'd feel big/ "Just more poetry about the patriarchy" I said / laughing in my

nervous reveal/ despite the fire in my belly/ which was roaring/ which was raging/

He sat up/ reaching for his pants he asked, asked, "What's the Patriarchy" And I

looked at his chiseled back dense from lacrosse

as he pulled on his Ivy League sweater and his Nantucket Reds/and I thought about

his hedge fund job/ and the way he voted/ in the last election/ and our small talk/

which kept a lid

on my bubbling cauldron within/ and lying next to that beautiful man/ I had the stark

loneliness

of being with someone/ but not really with them/ at all / of someone's presence

making you feel so small

and it was/ then I knew/ that I had to stop sleeping/ with soul strangers.]

Martha's Vineyard, Winter, 2014.

Something Has Changed in Me Since You Changed.

"Something has changed in me since - since you changed," she said. We were driving on the twisted road behind her neighborhood, it was pitch black and a light rain had started to sift down through the headlights.

"It's not big. It's not big like your 'thing.'" My awakening. My family still didn't know what to make of it. It was still my "thing."

"Yeah?" I asked.

"Well I don't kill spiders anymore. My whole life, fifty years, I've screamed and then I've killed them. Now, now I still scream but I don't kill them."

I laughed. "Well that's good. That's a good thing."

"Yes," she said. "And I guess I don't kill other little creatures as well, either."

My heart welled up but she didn't like big displays of gush so I just looked out the window and said. "Well I don't think that's such a little thing. I think that little thing is a really big thing."

[Less focus on them liking you /More Focus on You Liking You. What you don't like about them/ Is what you don't like about you/ And what you like about them/ is what you like about you. It's all coming, everything's coming, from inside of you. She said, " I wonder why it took me so long to see That all that was ever looking back at me was me."]

Martha's Vineyard, Winter, 2014.

Swimming Lessons.

The Ocean as ever is the greatest teacher. I walked alongside her yesterday and she was just breathing, in and out, inhaling one wave to exhale another, and sometimes she's peaceful, sometimes hissing, and sometimes she's crashing, and sometimes she's roaring, just like Mother Durga on her tiger. Unruly dangerous free beautiful brilliant powerful and mysterious. The best kind of woman, in my opinion. But she's always breathing, a steady breath through all of her moods, taking it away to bring it back in new form. And I walked fifteen minutes toward the cliffs, alone, because my dog still can't really walk, it was the first one I've done without my fur companion since I re-landed here three years ago. And it made it all the more poignant, since we must, and we do, walk alone, people come and go into our lives, so do our beloved companions, but really, through this life we walk alone, until we can walk no more. And life always has ways to remind us of that, that this is between you and you, all of the battles and triumphs and failures and losses and lonely nights serve to remind you. This life is made by your choices. This is your journey, and yours alone. Even after loss, this mysterious show must go on. I walked, my feet sinking into the sand, bare feet still in nearly mid November. And by the time I turned around, the wind at my back to head home, I looked down to find my steps were gone. Lapped away by her salty tongue.

In the fifteen minutes,

she had erased

all trace of me.

I was there- and then suddenly I wasn't.

"Just like that," I asked her?

"Yes," she said, "just like that."

[**NO MORE SLEEPING WITH THE SLEEPING.** She asked, "Darling how was your

date.

/I grimaced, "not great/ But it went.. late/ Even though I knew it was far from fate/

"Who was he?" she asked./ I said, "a pretty man with great hair, good teeth, a fancy

job

and a hole/ where his soul was." My face fell, "My heart was in hell, I think I might pick the pretty ones to feel pretty my self." She nodded/And I said, "I tried to show him my mind/ He only wanted to see my flesh/ I talked to him about my life/ But he only stared back blank faced/ as if there was something lame/ About this waking inside of me/ I knew to him this was just a game/ But still I tried/ Even while something inside of me died/ "So then?" she asked/ I lowered my head/ "So then we went to bed." She sighed/ "My darling my darling my darling/ girl of mine/ You didn't do anything bad/ But men who don't see you / will only make you sad/ when they don't see you at all/ they'll only make you feel strange and small/ Please tell me that was the last time/ You sleep with someone who's still asleep/ Promise me promise me darling girl of mine/ No more sleeping/ With the sleeping."]

Martha's Vineyard, Winter, 2014.

Dying in Winter.

December was hard. I fell in Fall. I died in winter, as I always seem to do since my spirit became aligned with earth's seasons. This morning a lot came to me in between sleeping and waking, that time before the curtain rises. This thought came, one morning in that mist- time. "Treat them as if they've already died."

Perhaps you ask what that means.

My mother's death was my first real up close and personal encounter with death, the first death that tore my heart out. I beseeched the Universe for answers, plead with it for a bargain, a way out of the torture of regret: "If I had only done this, If I had only said this, if I hadn't of run when I should have stayed." Because I hadn't acted, when I had my last few years with her, as if she was really leaving. As if death was truly final. But when it did actually happen, and she truly left, and I spent months on my knees, maybe years. How could I have avoided this searing regret? How could I have known? Why couldn't I have treated her differently? No answer came. I just kept crying, "please just give me one more day with her. I would give my life for one more day." Then I even just begged for one more hour. I still ask, for just one more hour with her, to show her how much I loved her, and breath her in, hear her laugh. Sleep on her lap with her fingers in my hair. When death is at your door or your loved one's door, every second becomes gold. When we forget death, we spend hours, days, under the covers in self pity. At least I do. That's no way to live. That's a way to die.

And then the answer seemed to have come 17 years late this December. You see, death is real, and it is coming for all of us. If you treat everyone, especially the people you love, knowing that, that they will die, and then, as if they already have- feel the searing pain of losing them, grieve them, think of everything you might regret saying or- not saying. Then comes the alchemy. When you are with them again, every conversation, interaction with them is just a miracle-

a back from the dead-for-a-day gift, things shift.

And then walking on the frozen lake the morning those words came, "Live as if you have already died," filled my head. This day is just a bonus, a moment you could come back and do things differently. See things differently. Ask the questions you wanted to ask. Say the things you wanted to say. Yesterday was the day you died. Today is the day you wake up and live differently.

If you treat yourself like you have lived and then died- but were given a chance to come come back, by some miracle -choose to love yourself with that radical self love that is blooming in you, live the way you always wished you had. Tie that in with treat everyone like they've already died, and you've had to lose them but now you get a second chance to shower them with love- and the whole experience becomes one trippy choice-filled awe inspiring gift. Which, which of course it is. But we're human, so we forget. Today, don't go back to sleep. Don't forget. Treat everything and everyone as if you already lost them, but then were given one more moment with them. Forgiveness comes in, lands on golden wings. You unclench from that anger and blame in death, you have to let it go. All that is left is the love you felt for them. Love is the only thing we take with us.

Treat your house as if you were walking through it for the last time, then close your eyes, then see it again for the first time. Pet your dog like it's your last day together. Look at your self Look into your wyes. Touch your own flesh. Come home to your self, for once, finally. End the inner war in serene surrender. It's the last day in this body in this incarnation. Let that love fill your heart. Let it explode inside of you. And then realize- you get a little more time. To do what you dream of truly doing, despite what anyone says. Despite what your own fear says. To love the people you love. To treat yourself like the innocent child you are. To treat them like the innocent children they are. What a gift.

Treat life like you already lost it, but were given one more day. I wish I had done this with a few choice people, treated them like the gifts they were. It would have saved us a world of pain, because the little things fall away. Love takes the stage, fills the big roomy spotlight. Gratitude hangs in the air, Grace fills every word. Try it and see. If you get one more day with them, one more hour with them. One more day with you, one more hour with you. What would you do, how would you be, what would you say.

What. would. you. do.

[**RULE BREAKER RISK TAKER**. Every time you feel like you're breaking a rule/ ask yourself/ who gave you that rule. Don't be a worrier/ Be a Warrior/ Don't be a princess be a priestess.]

Martha's Vineyard, Winter, 2014.

The Spiritual Gym.

The way I see it we're in a big Spiritual Gym. The way to build muscle, to get stronger is to approach your fear, like the machines in those gyms I used to haunt when I was only focused on the outside and not the inside. But in this gym, it isn't "I've got some fat to burn," it's "I've got some fear to burn." Some fear to work through to work out to walk through. I'll meet you on the other side. If I want to get stronger, I walk toward it. And I exercise it. I exorcise it. If something scares me, I know I have to move toward it. When I hear myself say "Im scared," I reach for my own hand, and get the flash light out, and say "You're ok - Let's check it out. Let get up, super close, in the face of these ghosts."

When I was a little girl, I was scared of the boogeyman under the bed, and the monsters

in the closet. Now that I'm a woman, and a Mother to Myself, I can turn on the light and say

"Let's look at it." This is A Monster Free Zone, I will get down on my knees, and look under the bed for you, and give you the ALL CLEAR so you can sleep.

And every day, this is the practice. Everyday we gotta work out. We gotta look under the bed and say, it was just your fear telling lies again. Everyday there is a new fear to be exercised, to be exorcised. Every day move closer to something that scares you

and kill it with love.

[She said, "darling its really ok/ to grow out of the skin you're in/ it feels like a death but its really a birth/ just lay back on the river / and let life take its course."]

Winter, 2014. Martha's Vineyard.

Re-claiming the Word Witch.

I cannot imagine anything more important to this culture this time on the planet or to me personally than re-claiming the word Witch. I believe that magic and miracles are all around us, for those who are looking. And don't you think this world could use some magic and don't you think this world could use some miracles right about now. I don't hex, I don't sacrifice. I honor the earth. I am aligned with her seasons and the phases of the Moon. It's She and we who have been sacrificed. The earth, healers, the deep feminine, the wild and wise women aligned with her were hunted out of patriarchal society. [I beg of you to look back at the witch hunts, so you can see the hunt was just on the Feminine itself]. The soil is dense with the blood of the feminine. You can kill a body, but not a soul, and the souls of the witches are rising. Cant you feel it? The world is asking to be returned to the hands of the healers. There is nothing more important to me than reclaiming this word, so people will have to look at it, and see what it really means, which is a wild woman, which is woman of the earth, who speaks for the earth, and what could be more important than the voice of the earth right now. The word Witch was the gateway back home to my self. It's my journey it's my truth it's my soul. Witch. A woman of the earth. The voice of the trees, wind, water, animals, earth. Witch."

A woman was tried as a witch if she/ spoke her truth/ lived alone/ owned land the government wanted

/ looked at someone the wrong way/ worked with the earth/ her neighbor got sick/ was devoted to the earth and not a Patriarchal God/ was too beautiful/ was too ugly/ was too sexy/ was too smart/ was too powerful/ didn't fit in/ believed in magic/ healed herself others and animals/ loved the wrong man or woman. These were your ancient sisters. This is the karma many of us are awake and here to heal.

[WITCH. A woman who is aligned with her ancient nature. A healer. A wise woman. A co-creatrix with the Universe and a believer in the magical sacred divinity of herself and all beings. An autonomous woman who aligns with cycles, seasons, and power of the earth and moon through ritual and communion. Her body and Mother Earth are one. The moon speaks to her the trees speak to her the animals speak to her the ancients speak to her and the Goddess lives within her. Her power is Love, her oneness is with nature and all of her creatures. She was once hunted for her powers but at the time of the Earth's greatest need, now she rises."]

[You didn't kill me/ you only made me stronger/ and I cant stay small for you / any longer].

Martha's Vineyard, Winter, 2014.

Relapsing to Remember.

I relapsed over Christmas and had a few glasses of wine. It wasn't terrible, it wasn't wonderful, it just wasn't at all for me. The only substance I'm allowed of late is the spirit inside of me. I had two glasses with a friend and wandered down an icy road to Main Street. We watched a puppet show. I'm not sure of what was happening, like good art it left a lot up to interpretation, it was roomy so others could crawl inside of it. But I know someone was in search of their voice, and when they found it it was like giving birth to a baby. I remember finding mine, when my soul woke up. "What do I feed this thing, and how do I care for it?" I forget sometimes we are our own children, what we feed ourselves we become, we still have to be really careful of what we take in. So be careful of the junk and be careful of the lies. And the more I read about Avalon the more I become Avalon and the more I read about ghosts the more I become one. I've been wondering if I am one again, Cathy scratching on Heathcliff's windows. But the closer I get to Goddess the more she reminds me I am doing as she does, dying in winter to be reborn in spring, dismembering to remember, deprogramming to reprogram. And, that makes soul-sense to me.

When you're in your underworld you don't make much sense to people on the surface. But you have to trust your own descent. You'll be back wearing her jewels. You'll rise with the gold from the wreck. You're down on the bottom of the ocean, in your own Atlantis. Those who can see Avalon don't understand, those who trust in magic and honor the cycles do. They let you go down all the way down. They know you'll rise as you always do. You'll rise wearing the Crown.

Spending so much time with Goddess you can't help but become Goddess. Half real half magic half death half life half dark half light half sun half moon. But don't try to be just one. Marion (Woodman) says if you try to be a Goddess all week you'll become the devil on the weekend. I know, I've been there. Don't try to be anything, just be. It's why you feel so good floating on the water in the summer. Half of you basking in the light of the sun, the other half caressed by the murky dark depths. And certainly stop trying to be what you already are, which is so much more than enough. You know that moment, we all have it, then we lose it, then we have it even more than before, where we say, "I've finally decided to just be me."

She wakes me in the middle of the night, I keep a pen on the nightstand for her. The other morning I woke and found I'd scrawled this on a book jacket: "I hope my writing will serve as the glue to help put you back together." Long ago the Goddess was shattered. Everyone of us that rises pieces her back together on the planet. We rise to the stars, feet planted firmly in the earth. We are the Grounded Feminine, and what could be more powerful than that.

[**I Tried That.**"Why don't you just tell him you love him,"she asked.

"Ive done that before," she replied. "With a man last winter. I put on silks and velvet and my best hat and I filled a glass with courage and I drank it down and I went out and let him know in the only way I knew." What happened?

"The next day I wrote a poem in bed about a warrior dragging herself out of a cave with the teeth marks of last night's rejection carved into her flesh."

"Heavens, that's dramatic," she said.

"Hell," she replied, "it was."

"Well has your heart healed?"

She surveyed her arms her legs and then she put a hand over the tomb that boomed. Scarred but strong it still beat, as loudly, louder, than it had before, like a hungry child, awoken from its slumber, it cried out for more.

"I suppose so."

“Well then I suppose it’s time you tried again. Because the longer you stay in here it would appear you live in fear.”]

Martha's Vineyard, Spring, 2014.

Valentine's Day.

She said, You call in the perfect partner by becoming your perfect partner. So I keep doing that for me. I bring myself coffee in bed. I light candles and run hot baths with lavender. I dance. I clean up after dinner for myself, playing Bonnie Raitt in the glow of the Christmas lights. I soften up on myself. I become what I want from him, hilarious and brave and fearless and confident and deep, sensitive and strong, artistic & activistic. I teach yoga in my living room. I take guitar lessons, and play, badly, but smile through it. I watch the cardinals land in the slush outside. The red in the vast sea of white is a witchy metaphor that Love can find you anywhere.

I saged her heart in yoga this morning. And then I saged mine. May the dead leave to make space for what longs to live. {We're three quarters through winter. Light and life are officially taking the lead. } Like helping spirits cross over into the light, my friends have gotten good at that. For everyone is talking about how their house gets so haunted on this island in the winter, all our ghosts coming out to play in the dark. I exorcise my heart. I remember how I never really knew what love was at all. How it's taken me four years to really heal from my great love shipwreck. We were given each others hearts, but we had no idea what to do with them. Babies trying to care for babies. Butter-fingered love football players. Bruising each other beyond repair, always dropping the ball and crying Foul. Love is a living thing, to tend to, to care for. We didn't know how to care for ourselves, let alone the love we'd been given. It is a language I am only just learning how to speak. How could we have known, if we hadn't have learned, so painfully. The lovers since him I've only played in shallow water with. I haven't dared swim out deep with them. God forbid I can't make it back this time. I barely made it back last time. I empty out the tomb that holds the old lovers to make space for the new ones. For the One I will love the way they long to be loved. For the One I will love the way I long to be loved. I learn how to love him by lovingly myself.

What is your intention for the day?

Radical Self Love.

She said what if instead of having a crush on another dude, You had a crush on yourself. What if you fell madly in love with yourself the way you fall so madly, in love, with them. What if you began a full on Self Love Affair. What if you saw yourself through the eyes of the Beloved. Be. Loved. What if you knew you belonged so deeply to this world it couldn't breathe without you that there was nothing you could do to make it un-love you. I said how did you know my secret that I have never really felt

like I belonged. She said its all of our secret. But the truth is no one

could belong more than you do. We all belong. Belong, in this very moment. She said take a deep breath and Come home. Stop wandering like a beggar. You are home. Relax into your body and drink the air like wine. You belong You have permission It is all green lights. Now what? This world responds to your every thought. Everything you believe you become. Everything you think about, you attract.

It took me until two days ago to process that, despite being told my whole life. Does it blow your mind, the way it did mine? I play a lullaby naked on the guitar- I remember I'm singing it to you, and my voice softens. I remember you, and I soften. I eat the chocolate chip cookies for breakfast, she brought me over for Valentines Day. They tell you to write love lists like ordering from the Love Diner. I realized I had never known my whole life

what I wanted until now. Because I had never really known me, until now. What's on your list, she asked and peered over my shoulder. She smiled at the big hands

and messy hair part and she said, You have messy hair, and little hands, and yours will fit perfectly into his. Then I said, I also want to be called His Girl. I always loved being called His Girl. I pull together old writings, painstakingly, like going though skeletons in the closet. My, how awakenings can be so messy and not flattering, that's right, embarrassing, it's wincing work. But I pull them together, anyway. I want to have something to show for all my changes. It's hard work, rifling though your closets of disaster and discovery, but I hear "Fuck it, Be Fearless," from the angel on my shoulder and I carry on.

I take a break from the work to write to you. I get so full of thoughts I have to lay down and birth them. The birds are knocking at my wooden door with their beaks, carrying a message. Death has knocked on many doors this winter. Everyone feels the chill. If you could do it differently, what would you change? I would be happier. I wouldn't care what they thought. I'd smile so big they'd have to wear sunglasses. I'd ride my broom through town in a velvet kimono. I'd raise enough money to buy a horse farm. I'd rescue every dog in the tri state area. I'd build a healing center by the lake. I'd hold free reiki clinics and teach self love yoga to teens. I'd hug those who call themselves my enemies and tell them how much I loved them and had learned from them, even though it drove them crazy. I'd play my bad lullabies in coffee shops, then open up a poetry circle on the stage. I'd take naps and not feel bad about it. And. More. The wind blows so strong, carrying trash can lids and tree limbs across the yard. The more wind, the more change. So much change on this day of Love. Love changes you. Are you ready, to be changed? Yes. I got too good at saying no. All that No hardens you and you forget to Let Go of who You thought you were. I turned them all away at my door. I say Yes now, instead. Life kept asking me to dance and I kept wall-flowering it. Arms crossed, waiting for a better offer than what was. What is a better offer than Now? Might as well dance. We don't know how long we get. Sometimes I think I only get ten more years, because that's how long my mother got. But it could be less. And it could be more, the only thing I'm sure of is I have right now. She asked when are you going to claim the life that waits for you.

I've watched people and animals and crops die without love. I will die without my own love. Everything dies without love. I've watched people and animals and crops be saved by love. I will be saved by my own live. Every time I seek outside of Love, I come back to Love, as the highest of all the laws, and the only religion, and always only ever the lesson. If you're wondering what the answer to your question is, it's Love. I've made some bad choices, I've followed my ego, and not my soul. Can I trust myself anyway? What's a warrior? Someone who gets up after they fell down. Someone who never stays down.

At lunch I'll eat the handmade quiche from a friend I had dinner with last night. I'll make a fire with the kindling her boyfriend put in the front seat of my jeep while she and I caught up, without my knowing. He said he wanted to make sure I was warm. We talked with the Olympics as background music about how last week was so hard we cried like babies

waiting to be burped. But this time, talking about it we were laughing. That's how it works. We were sad last week and this week we lived to laugh about it. Mantras come to me in my sleep. The only thing that is happening the only thing that is real is what's happening now. The other night it came like a Gregorian Chant. The only thing that is real is the now.

My bank account is empty. My heart is not. Being broke feels rather rich.

[YOU ARE A WARRIOR OF THE LIGHT. HEAL YOURSELF. FIGHT FOR LOVE. SAVE THE EARTH.]

Martha's Vineyard, Spring, 2014.

More Endings.

They told me when I came out my mother's stomach I came out crying, screaming bloody murder, I had ripped a clamp out of her incision, I held it high in the air in a tightly clenched fist..nurses came running. I made a BIG FUCKING DEAL about my first birth, and... I made a BIG FUCKING DEAL about my second birth. Cuz it felt important to tell it. And looking back, I would never be able to do it again, I would never have the guts to... spill my guts out, so personally...but isn't that what they say about birth, that it's so painful, that's why we forget. Because if you could remember it in detail you would never do it again. It was gory and humiliating and terrifying and visceral and amazing.

And it was a long three years in the birth canal. And it was a ton of digging out the grave I'd made for myself in my old life. And it was a bunch of swimming to a new shore after I dove off the old one. And it was a bunch of Kali scything away the false mes to get to the real me. Which she will continue to do, I just hope she never has to work as hard as she has the last three years- for her sake, my sake, the sake of others.

And, most importantly for me, because it's how I've felt my whole life, I broke the glass on this tomb I've been living in, the glass that separated me from life. And I took a big deep breath in, and I relaxed. And I received. Like Anais Nin says, "If I had not created my own world, I would certainly have died in other people's." I did die in everyone else's world and it's been three hard years creating my own world. And now I want to live in it.

The last few weeks I've been seeing suitcases. Like, I'm packed up and ready to take off on a new adventure. I'm tired of who I was, I worked really really hard to heal. And I hope, in the process, re-awaken the feminine and de-stigmatize the witch.

And now I'm open to who I can become. I no longer have the wounds, just the lessons. I'm lighter, I'm more open. I'm here. Joy and I are becoming bedfellows. I'm happy-sore from dancing.

I pass the torch of the rebirth – the destruction of the old life for the creation of the new, the life of purpose…on to so many beautiful men and women. After rebirth… comes life. Comes love. And more art.

I think, in part, I chronicled my awakening so publicly so as to prove that it was possible.

You can change your life.

And now, I say freely, I don't know. I don't know. I have no…idea what next, no assumptions, no expectations. Which means, anything is possible.

[**SHAKE YOUR SHAKTI.** She said, "this love-starved world could sure use a lot more Shakti."

So then she stamped her feet upon the flesh of the earth/ Kicking up dust raising the extinct and she beat her fists against the drum skin of her Creatrix belly/ and shook her hips furiously released all the stories/ unfurled her arms and opened her heart/ as wide as the sky/ and all the fear left with one big sigh/ then threw her head back and howled/ so loud/ at the moon that all the sleeping goddesses/ and all the caged creatures arose and awoke/ and cried in return "Is it time?" And she replied, "yes, darling wild ones of mine," and the trees swayed and the oceans swelled to greet her/ and then when she was good and done / she said "don't worry/ there's whole lot more where that came from."]

Martha's Vineyard, Summer, 2014.

Rejection.

I think of rejections like being re-routed. When a door closes, I don't bang on it, demanding it open because I had assumed, or wanted it to be the right door for me. {And why would I do this anyway? Don't we know from experience, that the louder someone bangs on our door, the less we want to open it?} No, I keep walking down life's hallway. The doors that are for me, will open with a loving knock. The doors that don't love me- why would I bang on those, God forbid they opened and I walked through? I think about how we resist rejection, our ego rails against it, but if again, and if always, we look to nature, nature does not rail against a re-routing. A stream that had been moving in one direction gracefully moves with the bend in a new direction, without demanding to know why, or shouting out that this wasn't the way she thought she had or "wanted" to go, and she doesn't either, demand to know what's beyond the bend in the new direction. A stream, a river, is carried in the faithful nature that she is always being lead home to the Sea. And when I am let go now, by something or someone, it is my practice to let go in graceful return, and to know then that I am being carried to that great Sea of Love, from which we are born, and to which we will return.

[Just you wait and see/ You're gonna make it out of this/ And you're gonna feel bullet proof You're gonna be flying/ without even trying.]

Martha's Vineyard, Summer 2014.

Softer Now and Softer Still.

People ask me why they are so tired. Everyone is so tired. Everyone is recovering from a convergence of chaos this past week, when the moon and summer's energy reached their peak. Now we move deep into the waning moon -the let go moon phase- when our energy drains with the moon's energy, when the fall chill dances its fingers along your neck and you can't help but think of endings, deaths and goodbyes, and the last of the moon's light drips into the sea like nature's great cauldron and it stirs with change. Our hearts are just like the moon, sometimes full, sometimes letting go, sometimes emptied to be full again. We walk the in-between bridge at the waning moon, between one phase to the next phase. It's a creaky, thin, dark little bridge that requires much trust. That Bridge of Trust we so often Must Walk. People ask in the dark, "what do I do," when the question is "how do I be?" and the answer is always open, and the answer is always faithful and the answer is always loving. When life gets hard, go soft.

[**FORGIVENESS.** "Thank you for forgiving me," he said. And she said, "I didn't do it for you/ I did it for me. See I was in a prison/ When I held the key/ And there was so much more/ Beyond your door to see / All along I had a radio station/ Only tuned to you/ One mere/ one note station/ When there was so much more to hear/ I unlocked the door/ I changed the channel/ I set myself free/ I didn't do it for you/ No/ I did it for me."]

Martha's Vineyard, Summer 2014.

The Less You Want to Fuck with It

I think growing up means taking your inner child to your breast and listening to her at all times, becoming your own mother, you stop asking for permission to live your life, and you you stop playing certain games.

My mother's Mary Chapin Carpenter tape sits in shredded brown ribbons in the bottom of my purse, I'm too sentimental to throw it out, I don't have much physical evidence of her left. But I thought to myself, "I played that too hard, and I broke it." And I thought about the games of love we play, "I played that too hard, and I broke it," "I pushed that too hard, and it shattered," and the games we play with others hearts, "I played that too hard, and I broke it," "I pushed it too hard and it shattered." And in my own definition of maturity, I'm not playing any games with love any more. I will play in the fields with children, and I will play in the water with my dog, and I will jump from a closet and still scare my sister to this day, even though she always feels it coming, but I won't play with hearts any more. Mine or yours.

The more you understand the power of the heart- that it is nothing less than the most powerful force in the world- the stuff of wars and Shakespeare- less you want to fuck with it.

[He said "*cant you just talk about the weather for once why does everything have to be so deep*" and she said "*I've tried that but the state of the weather leads back to how we've treated the feminine which leads back to how we've treated the earth. Everything leads back to this.*"]

Martha's Vineyard, Summer, 2014.

Brutal Gifts.

I'm thinking about the gain of loss, the brutal gifts, my mother called them, the boxes of darkness, Mary Oliver calls them. How I "have" something now that I once lost, and only because I've lost it can I know to be so tender and worshipful of it now- so moment to moment in awe of it- in a way that the first time around, well it would have been, was, impossible for me to grasp. It was as if, after watching someone you loved die, and mourning them for years, ruminating on what could have been, they arose from the dead. After years of shivering in solitude, a stranger in face but not in soul, walks up and puts his coat around your shoulders. "You came back," you say. "Shh," he whispers, walking you home.

This time around, they will not be taken for granted. This time around, you will say what you wanted to say, and hear what they have to say, and love them the way they should have been loved. The gain of loss. Someone once said the only way to keep it is if you give it away. How precious things become when we lose them.

I had to lose the gift to appreciate its enormity, for again how could we have known if we hadn't have learned. He once gave me a box of loss so brutal, but I opened it and I learned, and only by opening myself to it, peering into the dark tomb of me, for that box of darkness was my very shadow, that I did learn, that I do learn. Only in the dark did I find the gold of my soul.

The gift of loss. The gain of pain. Years later, wiser and humbled, both older and younger, I bow to him in heavy gratitude.

And I'm thinking about another box of darkness I gave to someone, my shadow, who gave me a box of darkness, her shadow, back.

And how "better" our lives are from something so "bad," how lighter we are, from something so dark, how closer we are to our truths, from a lie, and I'm thinking as always how so often the worst of life brings out the best in us that the "worst" things that happen to us so often

become the best. How we break down to wake up, how we die to live.

How death and birth could be one word, maybe "beath," one letter short of "breath," which is life itself, because a death always precedes a birth. The night is death and the morning is birth. Each morning, if we so choose, we can be new. Each night, if we so choose, we can let it all go. There is no one without the other, an ending is always a beginning.

[She said *One thing I know to be true*

the Tides will turn

they always do

and another thing

I know to be true,

is you'll make it through

don't you see

you always do.]

And this summer my yard is filled with children who believe in magic who catch fireflies

ride brooms and shriek into the sky from the tops of trees and yesterday the little girl and boy knocked on my door with an old cracked ball the size of a small fist they believed to be cursed. In the middle of something, although looking back what could be more important than playing with children, I told them to bury the ball and bury the energy and ask it to be transformed, and then I closed the door. But an hour later, when I was headed out, they were still by the burial site, the little girl writing letters to fairies for protection.

And they kept saying, "the curse, the curse." Impatiently, with reaction to the word, I threw a finger to my lips. "SHHH," and then I heard myself say,"The first thing to do is stop saying it, stop telling the story. The second thing to do is stop believing in it

never believe in the bad

only believe in good things- because believing in anything

or anyone brings them power. So don't believe in the bad, only believe in the good."

And the little girl looked in my eyes and we both understood.

[**TOMB OF PATRIARCHY.** He shook her hand entranced and asked , "What is it you do, I mean isn't that what we're supposed to say?" She asked, "is it? I suppose I've forgotten the rules / of what I'm supposed to do, and what I'm supposed to say- Me- I unearth the wild woman from the concrete tomb of patriarchy, Day by day by day."]

Summer, Martha's Vineyard, 2014.

Turning a Corner

Two weeks ago it was if I had waded into the ocean and I knew where I was, I could feel the sand beneath my feet, soft but firm, it wasn't- I wasn't- going anywhere and then, but then.

I got swept up in these tidal waves of men and I went under. And if you're lucky enough to have people watching you on the beach they get worried- they could see you one minute, then one big wave took you and you were gone. Should they rush in and save you? No, I didn't need saving and no one but me could save me from this pattern. I've been in those black waves of my old patterns too many times, never to any good, to much destruction. But this time I'm conscious and that can make all the difference. The wrong man, my friend has told me many times, can be the end of you. And I knew that, I've lived that, but a small part of me still wanted the drama of destruction.

But then. Somehow, somehow I broke out of the pattern, of that rip tide beneath the waves I felt very certain this time I wasn't going to let myself drown for lust or one sided love, I wasn't going down with this ship, this time I'd hold my ground for true love. Even though there are times I just wanted the waters to take me, but I've done that before, and I almost didn't make it back, so I clawed, tooth and nail, out of the water, back to my path, back toward my golden throne on the sand. And I emerged, exhausted, from the battle with the lifelong riptide, back to myself.

I didn't let it take me fully, just the part of me that always lost herself to men, as there had been a whisper from deep below, "lose your self- no really, lose the self you identify with so tightly, the one who tells the story about who you are in love, the one about you and bad boys and always getting wrecked and left." And I let those old patterns get rinsed out in the spin cycle of the waves, and I emerged, washed clean, buffed by the same forces that turn sharp breakable shards into soft eternal sea glass.

And the part of me that reemerged from the water

left all the bad boys behind for one. good. man. And carried away in the waves was the Little Girl who always lost herself to love and who emerged was the Woman who simply was Love. And I didn't fall at the boy's feet begging for love's crumbs. The man and I sat side by side, Throne. By Throne.

SELF LOVE SAVES. She said, "The days I don't love myself are the days I do the most damage/ Not just to myself/ but to others/ for when I cannot serve myself/ I cannot serve the other/ My work for the world/ is to love myself/ It is not just for me/ But for the Good of all/ Self Love is the Least selfish act/ on the planet."

Martha's Vineyard, Summer, 2014.

No Man Has Ever Touched Me There

I wrote a story about a woman, ravished from a shipwreck, sobbing on the shore where she crawled from the water. She couldn't speak, she just stared out to the sea, and beside her, scrawled in the sand, she had written only, "Touch Me." Many men walked by and touched her but she only sobbed more and shooed them away until she just grew lonelier, dying away to a husk, like the empty shells beside her. The more men that touched her, the more she cried out in tears, exasperating all those whose hands reached out to her body.

Until one day one man walked up, read the sign, read her face, read the sea from which she came, then walked into the water, and dove so deep that the woman thought he might never return. Finally he emerged from the waves bearing a barnacle-encrusted box, and the woman gasped, her eyes lighting back up with the hope of life. Then he fingered the lock, and she cried out. Then slowly slowly gently carefully he opened the lock, which sprang open beneath his touch, and then he reached in with a strong and careful hand, he took out her heart, she gasped as it began to beat in his palm, then he kissed it, and held it up into the sun.

The light and life returned to her body as he knelt down and placed her heart back inside the gaping hole of her chest. The blood of life returned, pumping through her veins. She opened her mouth and the words fell out, "No man has ever touched me there."

[She said, "Sometimes I feel just like dropping the ball/ And letting myself fall All the way down /A deep dark cool descent to the center/ Where I land naked and held in the palm / of the loving force that made the world/ I've been holding on so tight/ I feel like just letting go/ And exploding into a thousand stars of light/ I feel like taking a breath so deep

That I finally exhale and release/ All I ever forced myself to keep."]

Martha's Vineyard, Summer, 2014.

Leaving the Cage.

I know this is not a cage you've put me in, I know it's mine, my self - imposed cage. We cage ourselves into our comfort zones. We think we are protecting ourselves when we're actually imprisoning ourselves and cutting ourselves off from the true experience of life itself. There is no true safety in life, no guarantees except right now. It should be, as Helen Keller says, a daring adventure or nothing. My comfort zone is DOITGIRL. One time, a teacher told me a story about a prison being broken open by vigilantes. And when the freedom fighters came through opening cells, many lifelong prisoners were too afraid to walk free. They had grown too comfortable. And it was all they knew, so they huddled in the back of their cells and refused to come out despite life and freedom itself beckoning. The unknown was far more terrifying than their known prison. I think of everything as a metaphor, and this one is particularly potent for me at this time.

As wild women- if we are going to call ourselves that- we should walk as that-

We should always be looking for the current force/identity/thoughts and beliefs that cages us in. We should stay wild, outside of our cages. For me it's my handle my limiting mantle- an embodied woman wearing the name of GIRL- it's these titles of teacher priestess and... witch. All my labels limit me.

What cages you? The other night a man said to me as he wrapped up our conversation, "Alright, DOITGIRL." And I didn't realize how weary I was from carrying that identity. I shook my head, tired, like a mule having carried a tourist's heavy baggage up a winding Greek road. "No," I said softly.

"No?" he asked.

"No," I said.

"Then, who?" he asked.

"Sarah," I said, "whoever that is."

"Whoever any of us are," he shrugged with a smile. And all that freedom, all that unknown felt so exhilarating. I didn't realize I'd become so caged. For days after that conversation I was relishing in the deep mystery of life, which is the true nature of the feminine, which is life, which is MYSTERY. I was saying I DONT KNOW AND I DONT WANT TO KNOW! It was like skydiving, something I've always been too afraid to do. It was a free fall. Then I started to write as DOITGIRL again and the old feeling of confinement crept back in. My self imposed walls to this lonely castle I keep my heart "safe" in. Rumi 101: "Your task is not to seek for love, but merely to seek and find all the barriers within yourself that you have built against it." I cage me. I resist love. Because Love is the ultimate Mystery. And our work at every moment is to receive as much love as we can so that we can give as much love as we can. The more we love ourselves the more we can love others the more we trust ourselves the more we can trust others the more compassion we have for ourselves the more we have for others. I cage me. No one else does. And no one but ourselves holds the key to our own truth and liberation.

I'm seeking and by seeking I mean opening myself up to receive a better way to serve that serves me so I can serve on a higher level. Which means I'm going to have to walk down some dark hallways alone for a little while as I leave the seat of my comfort, and I'm going to have to take my own hand in the dark.

I'm tired of a fight that I don't believe should be a fight anymore. The Lover, she is so much stronger than the Fighter, she's softer, like water.

I remember bursting out of the broom closet singing it from the top of my lungs when I discovered my wild inner wise woman. But I believe the witch- a woman aligned with the earth and moon and her own intuition- should be a householder, as in, dare I say, NORMAL. Not a fringe movement. She stands for and is aligned with the earth, and there should be nothing crazy about that. {I don't think its crazy to want to save the world, I think it's crazy not to}.

I'm so tired of saying it but it will never not be true, as we heal ourselves we heal everyone around us and the earth itself, as our bodies and the earth are one. A fight for the feminine is a fight for the earth. And Magic- and my magic is Love- should be the norm. Fear should be what's crazy. Love, love should be the norm. So I'm going to stop talking about it for now and I'm just going to live it. As Paulo Coelho says, your example is much stronger than your word. Your walk is so much more powerful than your talk.

I'll always be aligned with the earth and the moon and ancient feminine wisdom will always be bubbling up inside of me. I'll keep writing, but in another form. This is the life of someone aligned with nature, changing as constantly as she does. Why is it so strange to be constantly evolving, when that's all nature is ever doing? She's never the same woman twice. Look around she is in a constant state of change and you are supported to do the same. When we don't grow, we die. Just like nature. When we get blocked, we get sick. Stagnancy breeds disease. Just like nature. {fear blocks us love moves us, to live, move}. We are one with nature. Look to her for all your wisdom. Love and nature are the same force and will offer you the same high wisdom.

I've had to fight so hard that in turn I became a fighter not a lover. I long to go soft and receive and open up to ever constant mystery. And being so aligned with nature it would be against my very nature and nature itself to fight during a time of earthly surrender as the wheel turns and the Equinox- a time to bury your past for good- comes quick on soft cool winds.

If I could offer you something it would be to love your present way more that your past. Treat the present like a lover who deserves your total presence. Tell it, I love you far more than my past. I am totally here for you, in this with you 100%. Choose your present moment and don't look back, don't bring the past into the present. Yourself Present moment is your life itself. Turning away from the present is turning from life. It's how we miss life and love, by lingering in the past. I love you dear present moment, nothing that came before you is more important than you. And tell that to your lovers too.

There should be nothing weird or fringe about a woman awakened to her feminine nature, aligned with the seasons of the earth and the phases of the moon. There should be nothing terrifying about the belief that- in a universe of polarity- God could exist in a feminine form. Nothing "woo woo" about being protectresses of the earth and a friend to all creatures. That just because nature and animals don't TALK doesn't mean they aren't in constant high level communication. That energy is the strongest language. Nothing strange about the belief that we have the power to heal ourselves each other and the planet.

And, I've been suppressing this other side of me, that just wants to write romantic comedies and have a baby. Did you know I was funny? Probably not, as there is nothing knee slap laugh worthy about death and rebirth and the suppression, or near extinction, of the Feminine, or the witch hunts, a gender genocide that caused women to hide from their true wild nature in a concrete Patriarchal world in an attempt at saving their own lives. Did you know, almost every problem is the world today is because of the suppression of the Feminine. But I'm tired. I want to write books in a silk robe with our baby on my lap and tea on the stove. And him, his heart as big as his vision, as big as his loving hands.

I have to allow space for that dream.

If I'm really going to walk the self-love that I talk I have to do what my heart calls for. If I'm really going to listen to the whispers of my own heart in a time of waning moon energy- a time of deep release- I'm going to let go of this identity so that it can transform. I knew I was being asked to let go something big but I never imagined it would be this big. It's time I practice the most feminine art of receiving. And only when I let go with total trust, of everything, when my hands are totally empty, can I truly embody the art of receptivity.

I don't think there's anything more that I fear than being a wise woman who doesn't take her on medicine so I've got to slow down turn in nurture myself and take my own medicine. It's not my fight anymore. The Goddess is back, and she lives in all of you.

Listen to the words of Mary Magdalene, Mary Oliver, Rumi, Hafiz, Osho, Maya Angelou, anyone who stands for freedom of the human spirit. But none could be more important that your own voice that shouts from deep within you, buried by all the external noise. Find her, uncover her from the rubble of the wars you've been fighting with yourself all these years. Finally end the inner war by falling in deep love with yourself. When you end the inner war you end the outer wars. When you are at peace with yourself you are at peace with the world. Take the little girl that cries out to you from deep within, take her to your breast and love the hell out of her, unconditionally. Show her the love she's been longing for. And may you never self abandon again. But if you do- rise to love yourself again, harder and softer and way way more than you ever did before.

[When were you born, he asked.

Right before she jumped into the sea/

She said, "that day I stopped pleasing them/

And started pleasing me."]

Martha's Vineyard, Summer, 2014.

Getting the Band Back Together

I was never very good at school. In fact when Shakti and I started teaching our Wild Woman courses together I had pain body memory through teaching. And we had to call it circle and gathering, to make sure the intention was clear. No one was higher, we were all one. This wasn't something you were going to be punished for if you didn't follow the rules. We were here to break the rules. Because look where all these rules have gotten us. We were sharing information that had awakened in us because it was our birthright and dare I say duty to do so and healing others heals us- no one was telling anyone what to do or giving them orders or rules. No hierarchy. Just. Sharing. Because when I was a little baby starseed I couldn't believe teachers could tell others what to do. I remembered a land where everyone was autonomous and equal. I was always raising my hand and getting kicked out for speaking my heart. The seat of teacher is a tricky one

You might have noticed I'm uncomfortable with labels these days, they allow for no expansion.

And in all this constant chaos of fall, we're changing as our lives change faster everyday. But I like to think of myself as a pretty good student of life.

I'm always asking what am I learning? Doing my best to bow to the lesson as threshold. What is God/Goddess/Spirit trying to teach me?

We know we are on the right path when our life is filled with synchronicities. Signs everywhere. Green lights. I know we have to let things go, for them to come back. I know we sometimes have to forget, so we can remember. And sometimes we have to take a step back from it to see what it is. I have always had to run away from home to miss it. I've done that since I was a kid.The response to me stopping doitgirl broke my big ass divine feminine heart

And when I stopped serving, I started dying. I didn't glow and I didn't hear God and I didn't hear Goddess

And nothing. Worked.

I was rudderless in the sea of life, I was like Darryl Hannah in Splash when they take her out of the water- to make her a "normal" woman.And she weakens and grows so tired and her beautiful glittery scales turn gray and peeling. She lost her magic. It's so tragic

When we lose our magic.

And then I realized Doitgirl isn't me, I don't have to worry about it being me. Doitgirl is the vessel through which I serve. It's barely a pen name. It was a credo given to me by God when I woke up. It was a call to shift the planet it was a call to rise. It was a call for the feminine to rise in balance with the masculine. For transformation

It's a call to arms, not the kind we shoot with, but the kind we hold each other with. For human connection. My story is your story, when we hear each others stories we become one.

I can no easier stop writing for God, as I can stop breathing. I am nothing without my service

I don't want ever to stop serving.

My addiction to symbolism and language rearranged DOITGIRL into GOD "LITIR"

Which is Gaelic for "letter." And when I first woke up I called these channelings "Letters from the light," Light, which is Love, which is spirit which is God which is Goddess

I could change DOITGIRL to GODLITIR but I'll humbly accept the name I was given.

Although I do love the hidden code within. I do love, hidden codes within.

So, Yes. As my friend Jesse said "Nice artist move, Sarah."

She said you're just gonna break up the band

to get it back together.

And nothing in me could tell her she was wrong. When I am quiet I am humbled.

Consider the band back together. Cue the music.

[I learned from the buck in the field last night. I learned that if I chase him he runs. If I stand there in awe, he comes. I learned from my dog this morning, that if I leash her she pulls away. If I take her off the leash, then she will stay. And I learned you cant give someone, something they don't want, something they didn't ask you for. I laid myself again and again at his feet, and he just stepped over me, and crossed to the other side of the street.]

Topanga Canyon, Fall, 2014.

Muted.

I want to write, I really do. But I feel like a mute with her tongue cut out. My power, my gift on the planet, feels gone for a spell, to see who I am when I'm not hiding behind the page. I barely can feel my feet on the earth, I barely, rarely, know where I am when I wake up in the mornings. "Patient," everyone tells me, be patient with this transformation. Like the leaves, quivering on the branches, your change is coming in the winds. I'm in that waiting room in Beetlejuice, between one life and the next, I'm in spiritual surgery, sprawled out on the table, they're taking out what I couldn't, what I didn't have the guts to or what I couldn't see myself. Goddess talks to me rarely, she just leaves the space behind my thoughts to quiet myself, to take my own hand, and I do, often, physically, take my own hand. I partially came here to this new coast for love, but that disappeared, like a mirage of water in the desert, as soon as I arrived, after crossing the states in my tiny red geriatric jeep, and taking two nights in a ghost town of Madrid, New Mexico, it felt just like a magickal trick brought me here, like Goddess was a magician, and he was her illusion.

"Now you see him, now you don't," She said, because the only thing that ever moves me is love, and she knows that. A man at the lighthouse on my New England island heard me talk about my winter move to the warmer coast. He said, "You either fell in love or have a broken heart. That's the only reason we leave here or land here." And he was right. I landed there with a broken heart, I left with a thirsty one. Here it's the wild open west, it's the great frontier, endless possibility is thick in the air but it's so hard without my furry familiar Gracie, who rests with my father in Virginia after surgery. And I felt like I had the key again, when she hurt herself and everything felt like I shattered, I remembered again, Fuck Everything That Doesn't Make You Happy. Because Your Bliss is Your Path and Your Path Serves the World.

But I wake up every night and feel her at my side like a ghost. Then the coyotes start to yip and growl in death council beneath my window, and I keep hoping they're killing my meekness, my smallness my old story and my fear. My friend out here, she keeps me big, when I try to play small. My hope for you is people who keep you big when you try to play small.

I try to keep these posts less personal, I prefer to Mary Magdalene my writing, to keep it like a mirror, with less detail, just enough so you can see my story is yours. It's my only hope at contributing to the healing of the planet, that I rise the feminine by bringing them out of hiding with my tales from the depths, my tales from my closet, my songs from my soul. The feminine energies of love and healing will save the world if it can be saved. All my friends out here are all healers, so I'm seeing it happen before my watery eyes. Everyone is rising into a healer, simply because this planet and its people need so much healing. This Love-Thirsty Planet.

So I prefer to write in the third person, as "She," and not "I," for haven't you felt the evolvement from Me, to We, but some things feel like they need to be said, like when people say, "See the World," they don't just mean the rolling hills of Scotland or the jungles of Costa Rica, perhaps they mean what I saw in Mexico last weekend, the babies in shopping carts, the dead dogs on the side of the road, the trash in the wilds and the people the people, with hollow eyes begging for food and selling puppies in the road. I had to see that too. And I had to not look away.

GIVE GOD BACK THE PEN. When spirit talks to me it is the same message again and again. To let life take me. To let life change me. I'm hanging onto the side of the cliff, white knuckling my life/ holding onto what I thought it had to look like and thought it had to be. I need to just let go/ and fall into life's sea/ Spirit took my tight balled fists of control and opened them up and said, "Give God back the pen. Release and let go. Give the greatest story teller ever, back the pen."]

Fall, 2014 Topanga Canyon, California

I Remember Avalon.

I have to remind myself, when money woes flare up, when the dentist appointments and errands and car troubles happen, you know, the everyday STRESS, I have to remind myself

THIS IS THE EASY STUFF

this is the tiny shit.

The real stuff is love and death. The real stuff is when people get sick and do battle with their own death and have to fight to be here. The real stuff is when someone dies before you get to tell them everything-- how much they're meant to you, how much you loved them, what was so wildly wonderful about them, how you thought of them every fucking day and dreamed about them. And then you never get that chance, in holy feeling flesh, in precious beating heart, in eye to eye soul to soul person. The real stuff is people's personal agony of not speaking their truth or living their dream or falling in love with themselves before they die, which can happen, all the time, young or old or somewhere in between. Self Love is a matter of life and death, I've found. Your work for the world is to Love Yourself. The real stuff is heartbreak, the real stuff is love, the real stuff is sickness, the real stuff is death. You are here to Live Your Dream. The other stuff, that's tiny shit. That's the stress that makes us sick.

There isn't some guarantee that we only die before we've found our soulmate or lived our dream. Did I once believe that, Don't Worry Sarah, You Only Die After You've Met Him and Lived a Long Lovely Life with Him with Your Perfect Children and Your Ten Best Selling Books at the Age of 88?

No, there isn't some guarantee we only die when we've lived a life we're satisfied with, like when it's "perfect." No this is it. We can die at anytime, with a life half lived, never having loved ourselves and lived our dream and forgiven ourselves and been kind to ourselves so we could do the same for others. The people we love can die at anytime, get hit by a car or slip in the shower or go to a doctor for something routine and leave with something terminal, and we could have missed the chance to tell them, I LOVE YOU SO FUCKING MUCH. YOU ARE PERFECT. EXACTLY AS YOU ARE.

And that happens all the time and I don't know why I, we, pretend it doesn't. Why we sit around and numb out and put the truth off.

The stresses, that's the small stuff. The heart of things, the heart, your heart, their heart, what your heart says, what their heart says, that's the real stuff.

When you get the urge to Love, yourself, anyone, someone, a stranger, someone you "should" be mad at or "shouldn't" love or "shouldn't" miss but your heart loves them anyway, act on it. Always act on love. Never act on fear.

What do I want to do with my one wild and precious life? Love the fuck out of people and love the fuck out of myself and love the planet. Sing my song, loudly. From the world's rooftop. Not care that Joe from High School thinks Ive lost it, cuz Im all about love and not fear, no sing my song loudly for the one woman I save. And no, Joe, I didn't lose my mind, I found my soul. I got blessed. I don't think I have time for anything else. I don't think any of us have the time we think we have. We get scared that people are going to think we are crazy, for living the truth of who we are, but the people who think we are crazy for living our truths are living in their own fear. And we can't hold back because of three people who will laugh at us when there is at least one life to be saved by shining your light. And the people who laugh at your light, deep down they are begging to be set free. And unconsciously, what happens, is your freedom frees them. So you keep going. Not just for you but for them. They don't even know your freedom is theirs and it doesn't matter whether they do. Just keep going.

Why do we fight so hard to stay small. We are terrified of our bigness. Move toward that terror.

It's your duty, says Rumi, to respond to every call that excites your spirit. To eradicate the patterns that keep you stuck in your story. To look for the places we are too comfortable, and to break past them. Shake and wake. It's our duty to feel joy, the highest healing vibration because our vibration lifts the planet's vibration. And the higher the vibration the deeper the peace, the more the healing. Its our duty to be bigger today than we were yesterday, and bigger tomorrow than we were today. And by bigger, I always mean, have the biggest heart, have the biggest courage. It's our duty to love back this body that has loved us so much, that breathes for us in our sleep.

You know that gulp you get in your throat? You're on to something. You're on to YOU. You're crossing a threshold. Follow the butterfly, I might throw up feeling, it's a sign you're leaving your comfort zone. It's your duty to go into the caves you fear the most. To walk up to your lions with love. It's our duty when we have found ourselves again and again in unrequited love, asking him, "why don't you love me?" to realize thats a reflection of our own unrequited love within us of the little girl within us asking, "why don't you love me?"

It's our duty to stop everything and turn in and love her. "Little girl," I've imagined myself saying to my own daughter, "you are not leaving this house until you love yourself."

"Tick Tock," I said to Shakti, "Time is Running out, to Say Something Before We Die."

Alan Alda says when he doesn't know what to say or what to do, or if this is something he should really worry about, he imagines being on his death bed. Will this matter when I am leaving for good. What would I say to them, when I am seeing them for the last time. And the answer always comes.

People always say take your power back. But I know, having been there, that's frustrating for someone who doesn't know what her power is. You have to get really specific to unlock your powers. It has to alchemize over time. You have to let your myth unfold. And then when it's unfolded before you, act. Walk into the mystery knowing who you are. Mine, my power is my words. My power is my big white light soul. When I feel powerless, I use my power to feel in power. By using your power, you are in your power. My power returns me to WHO I AM.

When I'm in my power, I'm in my magic, and magic abounds. The synchronicities pick up, those signs we're on the right path. "When you want what life wants, synchronicity and magic starts to happen." Adyashanti

What is Your Power. When you use it, it will heal not only you, but others. When you use it, it will free not only you, but others. By healing others, by freeing others, we heal and free ourselves. It is my duty to look in the mirror, without make up, sleepy in the morning, all alone, and say By God Woman You Are Beautiful. Because when I love myself I love all women. When I love myself I love you. When I love myself I give all women permission to love themselves. And I when I love myself I love all the world. When I love myself I have all the love in the world to give.

I remember Avalon, do you? Every single one of us served the Goddess within and without with a specific unique power. Our gift we were brought into the world to deliver. Do you remember yours? I remember the agony of not knowing mine. And now I know to know my gift, is a gift.

How does a Queen rule? By wielding her power, which makes her in power. What is your power? Only when we use our power can we be in our power. And only when we use our power for good, and with great love care and responsibility. Our power is our sword. We cut the paths of light out of darkness for others to follow. Those who have battled great pain and darkness rise into the Great Light Warriors of our time.

If you can see it, you are it. You are Greatness. Your Body is the Temple of the Goddess.

I Remember Avalon.

Topanga Canyon, California Winter, 2014.

No One Has More God in Them Than You.

No one has more God in them than you. I see all this projection, I FEEL all this projection, that something we see could be outside of us.

"She's so beautiful, He's so cool, He's an artist, He's a real activist, She's got it all figured out

He is everything. I can't live without him."

But Love, Love is recognizing You.

Finding a piece of your soul you lost along the way.

Love is coming home.

Eckhart Tolle says to love is to recognize oneself in another. I fall in love a lot. I find little pieces of my soul everywhere, in a song, in a face in the coffee shop, in others writing, in cabins on the hill and the wind over the water. And I love it. Because they're a reflection of my soul. Hint: I love what I am. I follow the pieces home to make me whole.

I fell in love just this summer. He disappeared, but I kept the lesson. He was the mirror of the masculine within me, whom I love. He was strong and capable, quirky and artistic, he could quote movies on the dime and tell you what song Johnny and Baby finally kissed to, he could fix my car and calm babies and dogs, he held doors open for pregnant women and made the waitresses smile, he challenged his perceptions and ignored his plans for the call of adventure, he chose pleasure over pain and happiness over sadness, he chose faith over doubt and he was me, I conjured him up, the masculine of me. I loved everything he did because it was something I would have done. Everything he did or said felt so familiar, it was something I would do, something I would say. So when I lost him, I didn't lose me. Because he was me.

Shouldn't this call us to the truth? That we truly love ourselves in the most divine way possible?

No one has more God in them than you.

And the person I've loved the most in my life, well he was the most... Me. That's when I felt most home, finding me in another.

When I was waking up I found myself at a shaman's house in the Berkshires, I drove through the valley until I found a healer's sign and I just stopped and knocked. And I was telling him about my awakening, this Kundalini zip line I was on, and I was telling him I desperately needed to ground, to find the foot path instead of flying through the trees, that my heart, it was blasting open so fast I thought I might fly away and become an angel again, too soon, too fast, and I still thought i had to be a rock journalist, it was before I found the art of being me, and doing that, and I was like, wow, this is how I feel when I interview Lady Gaga, she just has all these ideas and she's just glowing alive and so crazy creative, and he stopped me and said

Hold up, he said, You Are Lady Gaga.

She's pulling from the same consciousness as you. Which is God, which is Love.

Don't you see, he said, if you love it, you are it. He said, that's all reflection. You love what you are.

Everything is a reflection. Everything on the outside of you is a reflection of the inside of you.

Everyone has the god seed, which is meant to bloom. Look to nature, everything is meant to bloom. And don't you think it's terrifying for those little seeds to push up through darkness, not truly knowing whats awaiting them, just that they have to grow and rise, don't you think it hurts to push open their buds to reveal their true selves, but growth is birth and before birth is death, it's all so gory and glorious.

And no one has more God in them than you. We are all a drop in the sea of God.

And my friend last winter was waxing magickal about David Bowie as a genius but I finally got to say don't you see, you are David Bowie.

If you can see it, you are it. If you resonate with it you are it. We attract what we are.

And when you awake to the God within you, you can see everything and everyone as God. Because you see what you are.

And my friend, the other day, romanticizing a man who made her feel this momentary union of Home, when someone makes you feel like you've come home, which is what we are all trying to get back to, you know, back to the Garden, the unity of wholeness, of oneness with all things, of sacred union, of not feeling ALONE for one god blessed second, the wholly feeling of being gotten, she was telling me how amazing this man was she had met, and I got to tell her, and by telling her telling me, because we're all this magical mirror for each other, that no one has more God in them than her. Which for a moment, she had forgotten.

And then on the massage table in the dark Sunday morning, my healer asked me to let go of the people I was still holding onto in my heart, and I was scared to do it, and she said,

NO ONE IS GETTING ABANDONED HERE.

And I said can you put that on a t-shirt, and then on every billboard in Los Angeles, and maybe the world, we both started to laugh, and breathe really deep, and really let go, because we can grow and bloom and change in our lives, but NO ONE IS GETTING ABANDONED HERE.

Because all fears lead back to the fear of death, and change is death of what we know, so it can be terrifying to our ego and our loved ones around us, but No One is Getting Abandoned Here.

And she reminded me how when we stop abandoning ourselves, we stop allowing ourselves to be abandoned, we take our inner child to our breast and we say

NO ONE IS GETTING ABANDONED HERE.

We can even say goodbye, for forever or just a little, but

No one is getting abandoned here. He can hold you, for a night or a month or a year or a lifetime, your head on his beating chest and his fingers tracing the bones where your wings once were, and it can feel like you waited your whole life and every lifetime before that to be with him again.

And then he can leave, just like that.

But no one is getting abandoned here.

[**An Inventory.**

There was the handsome musician. Who yelled and screamed his heart out. Our sex, at first passionate, eating each other's flesh alive, burning for each other, became drunken missionary or sitting on the couch while the TV blinked in the background. I loved him I loved him I loved him. I loved him so much I left myself until there was nothing left of me to love.

There was a New England farmer. His strong hands creased with dirt, a relationship to fill in the blanks left by those we truly loved, sex was a nightly ritual to fall asleep, nothing more.

There was The Man I Shouldn't Have. And my ship went down in that wreck.

There were the two Europeans. Our sex rough, the conversations sparring, and both said, both said, I don't think you know what love is. They were bridges to new mes, nothing more.

Then there was finally, no man left.

And at the side of this battlefield, waiting, waiting, waiting,

abandoned without hope in fetal position/ wasting down to nothing/ the way things

die/

the way they always die

without love/ there was me/ forgotten/ alone.

I walk to her, ashamed, defeated, and I take her up in my arms.

I'm sorry I say

Come on, I say.

Let's go home.]

Logan Airport,

Winter, 2014.

Move Them with Love

Do you ever think about how you got to this very moment you're in right now?

Traveling helps you step outside of your life and look at it through the lense of an

author, a pause between the turn of the pages. I'm leaving Boston because my

mother's family is there. I'm in an airport terminal headed back to LA because last

June I met a man and we fell briefly in love, just long enough for me to fly out and drive up the cinematic Rte one coast with him in a vintage convertible and make love in storybook Carmel, a love that could only exist in soft focus movie set conditions not rough and tumble unscripted close up reality.

He was a ruse by a Universe that knew what moved me like puppet strings- Love- a ruse to open me up, from bud to blossom, and I'm grateful for him as a catalyst. In the Hero's Journey there are always the catalyst characters, those people who appear just to change your life- then vanish. I should say I have much more compassion now, for that little bud being ripped open to bloom, I imagine she screams too as she is peeled open. My friend told me that plants too feel fear and love. I feel that now. One thing one person says can change everything. That everything feels everything changes everything.

But LA and subsequent events out there forced me to grow up and I'm rather grateful to be an adult. Children can be abandoned. Children can be sent to dark corners and told what to do. Adults can't be abandoned. Adults can't be scolded and forced to play small. I rather like being an adult. Adults can look people in the eye and say "No

Thank You" and walk away. Adults can be left, but not abandoned, for they can take care of, they can serve, themselves. Adults are responsible for their own choices, as much as there are some choices I would have liked to blame on others- and did- when I was still playing small. But back to love, love is what moves us. Or me at least. Burning desire. Fire, the great alchemizer, the agent of change.

The spring of my twenty-first year I boarded the train to New York City for my internship at Rolling Stone, the light traces of the Springsteen lyrics "I'm pulling out of here to win" still scrawled on my back by a friend at graduation, with a burning desire to drown in the world of rock n roll. I would leave NYC six years later in love with a musician- mission accomplished.

Love is what moves me. In my last week on the island in golden September I visited the lighthouse with friends of the family and the keeper remarked on my imminent departure. "You must have fallen in love," he said. "How did you know?" I asked. He said "we only leave here if we fall in love or have a broken heart, and we only come here if we fall in love or have a broken heart." He was right, a broken heart was why I got to the island. Now that I'm healed and not in love, the choice, at least in this moment, feels all mine.

Two more months in LA to bang out a ton of work, then back to the island which will serve as my home base. But travel- for reasons not of romantic love - but love of the world, call, cry loudly. Can your soul resist its call? Mine never could. What is there to be moved by if not our hearts? People make the great leaps of their lives by finally hitting that I couldn't ignore it any longer wall. They say, I could no longer turn away. I couldn't pretend I didn't hear it. I couldn't pretend I didn't see it. I couldn't pretend anymore.

I can't sleep until I meet my calling. These days, my head full of dreams, my heart restless like a hungry child, I can't sleep at all. We can do almost anything we dream of- I don't believe we would possess a dream we weren't capable of, I don't believe we would see something we couldn't be- but one thing I know is we can never go back. Going back is death. Life means moving forward. There might be safety and protection in the bud, but there's beauty and glory in the blossom. All those labels, they were fables.

These days I feel I have two options - slavery to fear or bravery in love. I choose bravery over slavery, even the days the prison of fear seems more appealing than the liberation of the unknown. Some days I realize I'm my own warden. And then I have to punch through the fear bars, reach down into the cell, find myself huddled in the corner, reach down, take my own hand, help myself rise, liberate myself. Because the bigger I am and the braver I am, the bigger and braver others can be. I found an old journal this morning and it said just that. It said "I've realized, the bigger I am, the bigger all women can be."

It's true every time I see a liberated woman secure in her wholeness, the torch in my heart blazes brighter. And with that torch, I can see clearer, I can see further, and only with my heart ablaze in love and bravery can I light the way for another. Which I believe, is what we're here to do. I can tell when a dream has died inside of me, it feels cold and old within my bones. I can tell a new dream has been born when it crackles alive with desire inside of me. We're in the depths of winter. Tend to your inner fire. Stay warm, my friends. Light the way in the cold and the dark. Move them with love.

[WHAT IF: What if we approached everything and everyone in his way: *"Thank you for the Opportunity to Practice Love."*]

Topanga Canyon, Winter, 2015.

From Inside to Outside.

I want to write to you, and tell you of everything, despite a large part of me that just wants to stay quiet while I change in the dark. I want to tell you of the shift that happened, like a death. And I know, from doing this now for a bit, that the bigger the death the bigger the birth. I've experienced nothing short of a shattering of my world and a strict ordinance from my soul and Spirit that I can never ever go back to how things were. And the way things were was a looking in that got so isolated and unsustainable that the prison walls had to shatter and I had to walk out. I "studied myself to serve the whole," as Ram Dass says, until it was no longer serving me. And when I am no longer serving me I am no longer serving you. And when I'm not true to me I'm not true to you. And when I lost the labels I lost the limits.

That Christopher McCandless quote, "Happiness is only real when shared," continues to stalk me. Oh how I romanticized isolation in the wild. To be a lone kimono-clad writer in the corner of the world. And what we think of we become. But I don't want to dream anymore.

"Happiness is only real when shared" is true. And I want to be true. And I want to be real.

And I want to be happy, for me, my loved ones, and the world.

And I want to be shared. And I want to share, from a place of joy.

I think the true service to the planet is sharing from a place of joy. When you find your true service your find your joy. When you find your joy you find your true service. But we are always changing, so our service and what brings us joy changes.

Late last fall I had stopped feeling joy, despite the apparent success of my path. And I felt like a fraud, sharing a path that had lead me to healing, but not to joy. Stop, I wanted to turn around and say to the women who followed me. Don't come this way. It doesn't lead to joy. Only follow the road to your joy.

Then that winter, right before the holidays, right before my birthday, Someone came along and showed me what true service was. He spent one night in my bed but he changed my life forever. It was a level of service I didn't even know was possible. But looking back I had been banging at a ceiling again. And he took an ax to the prison of my ego and my soul rose free once more through the hole in the sky of my world he had punched. He walked away, back out into his world of service, and I was left to die and be born, once again. And while he walked away and I whispered thank you for this death which was my birth. Yet again. How many lives can we have in one life? That is up to you.

There comes a day in your healing you can no longer look in, you must look out. This was always going to happen, I knew it on a cognizant level but not a soul level, that once a woman heals herself, she then heals "the world," by that I mean the world outside of herself. She heals the inner world, and then moves to the outer world. She heals the wounds of her body, and then moves on to the wounds of the world. The Dali Lama said, “The Western Woman will save the world.” But first of course, she has to save herself. And I did that. I unearthed myself from the tomb of patriarchal society, and I claimed the power of my beating heart and I healed my wounds and now, because I, as a Western Woman, am one of the last on the planet with the luxury of time and resources to heal herself, I am ravenous to direct this healing energy elsewhere in the world. To break the wall, become a bridge, between my sheltered self and a world on fire. Offer my back as a bridge into the wounds of the world. The deeper our giving, the deeper our living.

Looking in now is almost impossible, painfully constrictive. Thoughts of and connections to the Other save me. When the Maiden heals herself she becomes the Mother. The Maiden, like a seedling, had to push up through the dark earth in her hard bud to break out to where she is free. First she has to declare herself and her voice and her autonomy. When we find ourselves there is a period of ecstatic BE-ing. All Feminine. And then she dies to be born again, to be torn open by the world and to offer herself to that world. That breaking of the hard bud is the breaking open of a woman's heart, and a broken open woman's heart is the power of the feminine that will heal this war torn, love thirsty world. Then we balance, we become whole, and we both Be and Do. For the Other. Which is the Self. Healing the Other Heals the Self.

And when she is broken open, then she truly receives. And when she receives, she has something to give. And when she gives, that is when she truly lives. She becomes a Mother to the Other- that sacred word buried within- a seed within the word "Mother."

Nothing that she can buy or drink or eat can fill her now. The only thing that can fill the hole within is to give. As Bhagavan Das says, "there is nothing left to buy."

All her life the only thing that ever alleviated the Western Woman's depression was Action. To take action to save herself.

Now healed, the western woman takes action to save the world.

Now she is urged to act-ually become action, itself, now that she is love itself she must put herself into action to become an Activist. Love in Action.

If she can do something, she simply must.

All this highly transformative energy, the energy of the feminine, which is Change Herself, she has used to heal herself, to change her life, is now focused on the world, to change the world. If she changed her life, she realized, she can change the world. If we can heal our lives, we can heal the world. My body and the earth are one. There is nothing outside of me. I am the other.

To die to the I brings unity, humility, humanity, it shatters the glass between you and true life. You leave the bunker and return to the front lines of life. Plato talks of this, of leaving the cave, which is the shadows of one's own mind, and moving out into the light, into the world, into service and surrender. I must keep walking, out.

I was the hurricane, now I want to be the shelter.

I've spent four years sharing my story with women internationally, and seeing truly, in the ways of Mary Magdalene, that my story was their story and their story was mine. Our stories connect us and humanize us and I've seen this in miraculous and remarkable ways, that the mirror that causes miracles.

I have done moon circles and retreats and online courses and lectures and there is a common theme in Western Women which has risen.

"I have so much but I am still so unhappy."

or "I have everything but I feel as though I have nothing."

Nothing can fill them but giving. This is why they come for healing, to rise as healers, to be of service. Their soul knows service will save them.

I know the holy grail that makes us whole is to give of the salve that healed our wounds. First we must have something to give though, and that is why we take this journey deep within ourselves, to find our true selves, our true purpose and to rise with that gold, the gold of our soul, to offer it to a dying planet. We ourselves are the healing elixir for a dying planet. And the first step is to heal yourself into Love, and then you walk as love into the wounds of the world. Everything Dies without love. But everything Lives for and Because of Love. And Love Heals All. When you are Love in Action you can save the world.

Death is my teacher. You might have noticed from my writing.

I pay attention to what they say about people after they die, what they say at funerals. And what brings loved ones solace when you have left is if you were happy.

They say, she lived a good life, she was happy. And that brings them solace that your life was not wasted. And if you die unhappy they say, "well maybe this is for the best, she wasn't happy, she was suffering." The measure of your life is your happiness. None of it matters if you're not happy. When you find what you love and you do what you love you are serving your purpose and God's purpose and you are ful-filled. When you find what you love you are serving the world. Your happiness- your joy - is your gift to the world. Only from our fulfillment do we serve. Your happiness is what you owe to others. A happy person expands and gives. A sad person shrinks and takes. Your joy is what you owe to the world. Your joy will heal the world.

I know my measure of success is happiness. So briefly, I feel like a fraud. It is why I have turned my porch light off for a bit, to finish culling these diaries, release this part of my story, birth this part as my piece in birthing the new earth, so I can live my next story, which is active service.

I used to think my mother's last message to me, "Find the Joy," she said, as she slipped from this world to the next, was just for me. But now I realize, moving into my own mother stage, creeping ever so swiftly to the age she was when she died, and seeing the world from a mothering, othering, lense, it might've been for her, as well. To find the joy for her, as well. My mother, first broken hearted, then sick, spent a large time in bed. Which came first, sadness or sickness, it doesn't matter they were one in the same. And so have I, spent too long in bed, even as I write this, I write from bed. Exhausted. And so have the women who write to me. They feel hopeless. They see no change in their lives. When we don't think things will ever change, when we feel stuck, doomed to repeat the doom, in our lives and in the world, which are one, we grow despaired.

But when they do see change they feel alive and empowered- thrilled to be awake and on their quest. Imagine if they could see their own effect of changing not only their lives but the lives of others, through their direct action.

I look around me at all these women rising into healers. It is happening, this is happening. The feminine is rising into action to heal the world.

In service, I drink from the holy grail of joy. In my purpose of service, when I see change in action, I rise empowered in the morning, I bloom like the rose. My blood and fire pumping red hot like the robes of Mary Magdalene. In service, from that endless cup of joy flowing over, I can serve. I have something to Offer the World.

The world is ravaged by imbalanced masculine energy manifested in ego & war. This is why we need the healing of the feminine to rise up in balance, and the work of the Modern Priestess is to balance the feminine and masculine within and without. She marries her loving dreams with action, making her whole. Her wholeness becomes the world's wholeness. Her change is the world's change. As she becomes balanced, as the people become balanced in masculine and feminine, so does the world return to harmony, like the sun and the moon, like day and night.

She heals herself with love to become love.

You are love now.

Act.

[The Brave Leave the Cave].

Final Essay. Taos. 2015.
Changing Rooms.

When my mother used to take us (I'm a twin) to the mall for clothes, we refused to change in front of her, we changed in the privacy of that little curtained stall, the Changing Room.
Still, she would try to peek as we slipped off our old clothes and stood, terrifyingly, repulsed, naked in front of the full length mirror, under its harsh bright lights that revealed these bodies that were rapidly betraying us. We bore new fat rolls and unwelcome horrifying hairs and breasts that were misshapen, the left was a B, the right was an A, and I had no use for those but shame, either.
(Once, with my frizzy, manic-panicked purple hair, plump body and braced faced teeth, my mother stroked my face and told me the story of the ugly duckling who transformed into a swan. When my sobs grew even more uncontrollable ("SO I'M AN 'UGLY DUCKLING?'", she'd console me with "Winona Ryder wasn't popular in school, but Vanna White was."
"Tell me that again, Mom," I'd ask, after a particularly bad day.
My mother was cool.)

My body changed every single day, like the trees outside, and I would stare at myself in the mirror of my bedroom, my walls plastered with Eddie Vedder and Helena Christensen, and I would try to see my future in my eyes. "What's going to happen to you?" I would ask, and pray for an answer. (Oh Please something good and wild and exciting, I want to see the world, and please may I fall in love, and can he look like, can he be, Eddie Vedder, or I will take Michael Hutchence.)
Everything was changing, right before my eyes, and I had no control. Over my body, over my anything, over my life, which was falling apart like a sand castle taken by a violent wave with my parents' divorce and my mothers' earth shattering cancer diagnosis.
But at least in that GAP changing room I could send the sales girl away, and tell my mother not to look. Now, we change in public, awkwardly between old Yous and new Yous that we don't quite know how to fully wear yet, You's that haven't totally been born, that form as you think and breathe.
I'm stepping into new jeans. They don't quite fit yet. They are awkward and uncomfortable but by god at least they are new. But these new jeans have pissed some people off, and some just cant stand to be around me in them. I get it, sometimes neither can I. I'm awkward and unpleasant sometimes, fussy like a new born baby.
I'm half formed, graceless in these new jeans which I can't even describe because I can't really even see them yet.
But I wear them, because I couldn't stand my old jeans. I could no longer wear those old jeans for one more minute. I really deeply outgrew them, they no longer felt like mine, they cut off my circulation, I couldn't breathe. I dropped them off at Red Cross in the middle of the night and said God Bless you thank you for how far you walked me but i MUST release you with love.
But with the release of the old jeans, you lose some people. You could even lose everyone. That's the risk you always take, it's why change is so terrifying, its the death of what we know. So you're choosing between the

path you know, which you can't take one more step on, and the unknown. And so you walk into the mist, and you disappear, and the only way the path appears is by you taking each step into the dark. You take one step, and the next one appears.

You do not find these new jeans in the Pleaser Section. And you know that recently people are thinking of you, "Well that wasn't very nice." And you used to be so terrified of not being thought of as nice. But a teacher once told you, that Love isn't Always Nice. It's true. And Nice certainly isn't always love.

Because Ive been nice, but I wasn't always telling the truth. Being nice meant ignoring my intuition a lot, even lying. then no one won. We all got hurt. But I was too nice because I wanted everyone to like me, and I just didn't want anyone to be mad at me. Because then I would have to feel those feelings.

For the first time in a long time, after years of spiritual dormat-cy, I could be seen as a bitch. I had to reclaim the word. I thought of a female dog, then a Mama wolf, who protected herself and her own. Well isn't that exactly what Dr. Pinkola Estes says a healthy woman is? ("A healthy woman is much like a wolf: robust, chock-full, strong life force, life- giving, territorially aware, inventive, loyal, roving.") Would you steal from a wolf? Would you cross her boundaries? I would respect the HECK out of a wolf. Above all, because a wolf respects herself. She would teach me that by walking it, not by talking it.

But shedding skins isn't fun. I think of the snakes in this desert here, I think of them, wide eyed, as the dress they've worn that has protected and identified them, slips off their body and they slither naked and vulnerable and nameless through their treacherous world.

People will leave you when you change. That, and all the discomfort & gnarly unknown & emptiness, is how you know you are changing.

They will fall away with the skins. And you will look around you, like the clothes in heaps on the floor of the changing rooms, all the clothes that didn't feel good or fit, and one of two friends who still talks to you in your

unpleasant changes will tell you, if you weren't shedding these things, how could you know you were changing?
And that will bring momentarily solace, and then you will cry again sitting alone in the living room, staring into the soulful eyes of your dog, who wonders if there is anyone she should call, but you have answered the calls of everyone who could understand, which isn't many. And those people know, you need space, those people know, "she's dying/changing again." And they know that the caterpillar doesn't change in front of everyone, she just changes alone in the dark in front of God, in her own tiny changing room in the corner of the world. All the great changes take place in the dark. In Changing Wombs.
So you wait. And you breathe. And you watch documentaries on people who inspire you. I spent the last three days in bed with Jim Morrison and Bill Hicks and a book about Sassy magazine.
You realize your cup is empty again. The Chalice of You, is empty again. And like a lost pilgrim on the road home, you need to find the River of Love again. You know that when you get lost you have stopped following the river of what you love, your river of joy. So you write down what you love, and that forms the river, and you know you have to sit by the river and fill your cup again. Only then, can you offer anything to this world.
It's like,
The old world I created, I couldn't live in it anymore.
And The new one, the new life, I'm still searching for the door.
"She's in between sizes," my mother would tell the GAP girl as I glared, embarrassed, at the floor.
I still show up, the best I can, when I can. But I can be terribly awkward. The swan mid transformation. I can put the ugly in duckling. (Sometimes, it is out of storms that we are transformed. Out of storms, we are reborn.)
And Other times I wish I could ask everyone in my life to go away as I change, but just like I would hiss at my mother at the door of the Changing Room- "leave me alone," I would say, "but don't go anywhere."

Go away, but not too far. I still needed to know she was there, hovering behind the curtain. I still needed to feel her, to hear her breath. Don't look at me, in this awkward dance of transformation, but stay right here, so I don't have to call out for you, or God Forbid, waddle across the floor of the store in front of strangers in these too tight jeans to ask you how I look. And she would always, always, tell me the truth, for better or for worse, for sting or for sing.

(And I used to pack a bag to run away, but I really only needed to cross the street, just to know I could, to cross a boundary, to feel free. To remember why I loved what I had. To miss it for a moment. To step outside of it to see it. But an hour

a later I would come crying into the house "Why didn't you come after me?!")

Now I change, now we change, all the time, in front of people, awkwardly, uncomfortably, looking back at who I've been (wince) and I'm convinced it's why so many of us don't grow, for first we have to look at who we are and how we've been, and fuck, what we've done. We have to look in that awful full length fluorescent lit mirror that reveals all. It's hard enough when it's just you looking in.

But they don't have to like you, you have to like you. And now I see the girl who twenty years ago stared into the mirror wondering what would become of her. She used to think it was up to the world, to give her what she asked for. Now I know it's up to me.

Four years ago, almost five now, I went through a rabid public spiritual awakening, one I wanted to shout about from the rooftops of the world. Now I go through an intimate fragile human awakening, one I just want to whisper about, in the dark, to that one other person.

Vol. 1, FIN.

LOVE ON.

Sarah .

19656190R00183

Printed in Great Britain
by Amazon